THE
BIPOLAR
HANDBOOK

THE
BIPOLAR
HANDBOOK

. . . .

Real-Life Questions
with Up-to-Date Answers

. . . .

Wes Burgess, M.D., Ph.D.

AVERY
a member of
Penguin Group (USA) Inc.
New York

Published by the Penguin Group
Penguin Group (USA) Inc., 375 Hudson Street, New York, New York 10014, USA •
Penguin Group (Canada), 90 Eglinton Avenue East, Suite 700, Toronto, Ontario M4P 2Y3, Canada
(a division of Pearson Penguin Canada Inc.) • Penguin Books Ltd, 80 Strand, London WC2R 0RL,
England • Penguin Ireland, 25 St Stephen's Green, Dublin 2, Ireland (a division of
Penguin Books Ltd) • Penguin Group (Australia), 250 Camberwell Road, Camberwell, Victoria 3124,
Australia (a division of Pearson Australia Group Pty Ltd) • Penguin Books India Pvt Ltd,
11 Community Centre, Panchsheel Park, New Delhi–110 017, India • Penguin Group (NZ),
Cnr Airborne and Rosedale Roads, Albany, Auckland 1310, New Zealand (a division
of Pearson New Zealand Ltd) • Penguin Books (South Africa) (Pty) Ltd,
24 Sturdee Avenue, Rosebank, Johannesburg 2196, South Africa

Penguin Books Ltd, Registered Offices: 80 Strand, London WC2R 0RL, England

Most Avery books are available at special quantity discounts for bulk purchase for sales promotions,
premiums, fund-raising, and educational needs. Special books or book excerpts also can be created to
fit specific needs. For details, write Penguin Group (USA) Inc. Special Markets, 375 Hudson Street,
New York, NY 10014.

Library of Congress Cataloging-in-Publication Data

Burgess, Wes.
The bipolar handbook: real-life questions with up-to-date answers / Wes Burgess.
p.   cm.
Includes index.
ISBN 1-58333-249-9
1. Manic-depressive illness—Handbooks, manuals, etc.   2. Manic-depressive illness—Miscellanea.
I. Title.
RC516.B87   2006   2005057210
616.89'506—dc22

Printed in the United States of America
5   7   9   10   8   6   4

Book design by Amanda Dewey

While the author has made every effort to provide accurate telephone numbers and Internet addresses at
the time of publication, neither the publisher nor the author assumes any responsibility for errors, or for
changes that occur after publication. Further, the publisher does not have any control over and does not assume any responsibility for author or third-party websites or their content.

Neither the publisher nor the author is engaged in rendering professional advice or services to the
individual reader. The ideas, procedures, and suggestions contained in this book are not intended as a substitute for consulting with your physician. All matters regarding your health require medical supervision.
Neither the author nor the publisher shall be liable or responsible for any loss or damage allegedly arising
from any information or suggestion in this book.

Manic depression's touching my soul.
I know what I want, but I just don't know how to go about getting it.
—*Jimi Hendrix*

Contents

Introduction

Yesterday, a woman named Susan found out she had bipolar disorder. She, her family, and her friends rushed to the bookstores and the Internet to find answers to their many important questions about bipolar illness. Unfortunately, what they found told them more about problems than solutions.

My patients asked me to write *The Bipolar Handbook* so they could see the answers to their questions in a book that they could take home to read and share with their families and friends. Boyfriends, girlfriends, and spouses asked me for a book they could give to their partners to help them understand what it is like to be bipolar. Doctors, nurses, and therapists asked me to write a book that they could give to their bipolar patients and families to help answer their questions.

Bipolar disorder is a unique medical disease that affects career, school, relationships, thoughts, emotions, energy, sleep, weight, and physical health. It is particularly known for episodes of either hyperactive mania or unmotivated depression, but many people have mixtures of these symptoms.

Individuals who suffer from bipolar disorder need two things: an understanding of their illness and practical strategies to get along in the world. Ever since I started my psychiatric practice, almost twenty years ago, I have been writing down all the questions asked by my bipolar patients, their families, and their friends. I asked other professionals what questions they were asked, and I scoured the Internet to find questions that had not been satisfactorily answered by patients' doctors and therapists. *The Bipolar*

Handbook is a compilation of those real-life questions with up-to-date answers gathered from modern medical and psychological knowledge and from my personal medical experience. No doubt, you will find answers to *your* questions here.

There are more than seven million adults and children with bipolar disorder in the United States. Politicians, celebrities, and members of your community are coming out and revealing that they have bipolar disorder. Many best-selling books are about bipolar illness. The news and the Internet are buzzing about bipolar disorder. Each year, I am asked to share my knowledge as a psychiatry expert on National Public Radio, on television, and in feature films. Old treatments are being validated and a range of new medication and nonmedication treatments for bipolar disorder is just becoming available. Both doctors and the general public are beginning to understand bipolar disease, and the long-lived stigma against bipolar disorder is abating. Now the world knows that many normal, successful, and famous individuals are bipolar and that they have found good treatments for their disorder.

I began my professional life as a scientist, studying the brain and behavior in departments of medicine and psychology at major universities. One day I felt a calling to change to clinical work so I could spend the rest of my life helping people with bipolar disorder and other illnesses. I completed my specialty training at Stanford University Medical School and served as a fellow at Stanford University and UCLA medical schools. Since then, as a licensed medical doctor and practicing psychiatrist, I have spent each day helping people with bipolar disorder and their families find the best ways to succeed in work, relationships, and family life. For the sake of my patients, I have to know what works and what doesn't work.

I wrote *The Bipolar Handbook* to be like a friendly chat with a trusted family physician who knows how to address your own personal worries and fears and who solves problems like yours on a regular basis. I want it to be as if you and I were sitting down and talking face-to-face so that I could give you individual counsel and cutting-edge information on the topics that you chose. I want the book to contain detailed information that has not yet reached textbooks, reference books, or the press, and yet still be easy to read and understand.

I want *The Bipolar Handbook* to give you options and choices beyond the same old theme of "just stay on your old medications." Most of all, I really want to stimulate your desire to know and find out everything there is about bipolar disorder.

My ultimate goal is to help people with bipolar disorder achieve their goals and access their special potential so they can live happy, fulfilling lives. It will take work, but the results are worth it. Let's not waste any more time.

1.

BIPOLAR DISORDER
BASICS

. . . .

We all have to become experts on bipolar disorder, if only because the general public knows so little about the illness. This chapter will help you understand the definition and symptoms of bipolar mania and depression, the different types of bipolar disorder, the causes of bipolar disorder, and the way society responds to people with the illness.

What is bipolar disorder?

Bipolar disorder is a disease of the nervous system that involves the brain and the body. Environmental, hereditary, genetic, and biological factors create changes in brain cells and an imbalance in the chemicals within the nervous system, resulting in abnormal fluctuations in metabolism, emotions, and thought processes, including attention.

What does the name "bipolar disorder" mean?

"Bipolar" refers to the two physiological states of mania and depression that are associated with the illness. These gave rise to the previous name of "manic depression." Although many people with this disorder have mainly manic or mainly depressive episodes, there is usually a mixture of symptoms at any given time.

Bipolar disorder causes much more than simply mania and depression. It can also cause feelings of irritability, anger, jealousy, resentment, anxiety, avoidance, embarrassment, fear, inadequacy, regret, and confusion. In addition to mood swings, you may experience drastic fluctuations in energy, activity, weight, metabolism, and the sleep/wake cycle. Bipolar disorder increases your sensitivity to stress so that you become more vulnerable to life changes.

Bipolar disorder impairs thinking by causing poor focus, distractibility, and poor memory. Poor judgment, impulsivity, repetitive, obsessive thoughts, and overfocused, compulsive activities make you more likely to overwork, overindulge, and take unnecessary risks. Problems with procrastination, poor motivation, and difficulty starting and/or finishing projects make it difficult to attain your life goals.

How many people have bipolar disorder?

It is estimated that 2 to 7 percent of people in the United States suffer from bipolar disorder. Almost ten million people will develop the illness sometime during their lives. About half of those will never receive the correct diagnosis or treatment.

How many people are affected by bipolar disorder?

In addition to the people directly suffering from the illness, bipolar disorder affects the lives of their parents, brothers, sisters, spouses, children, grandchildren, and friends. Parents struggle with the problems of bipolar disorder in their children. Doctors, nurses, therapists, and social workers devote their time to helping and caring for individuals with bipolar disorder. All in all, I estimate that about twenty million people's lives are touched and changed by bipolar disorder in the United States alone.

If I have bipolar disorder, how much of my life will I actually be sick?

Bipolar disorder is far more serious than most people think. One quarter of the people with bipolar disorder are unable to function for most of the year. Over half of diagnosed bipolar patients have four or more serious outbreaks per year, and some patients experience a mixture of symptoms continuously throughout their lives. However, this picture improves dramatically with successful treatment.

Does bipolar disorder cause physical health problems?

Yes. Persons with bipolar disorder have more heart problems than the rest of the population. They also have more headaches, particularly migraine headaches. Migraines are even more common in bipolar depression than in common, unipolar major depression.

Bipolar disorder also increases the risk for substance abuse and addiction: 60 to 80 percent of people with bipolar disorder will suffer from alcoholism or drug abuse during their lives.

Overall, the death rate is higher in people with bipolar disorder, especially those receiving insufficient treatment. Compared with the rest of the population, people with bipolar disorder experience more accidental injuries and deaths, particularly from motor vehicle accidents.

What is the worst thing that might happen to me if I have a bipolar episode?

The worst tragedy of bipolar disorder is that it can prevent you from having the kind of life you want and deserve. Without treatment, bipolar illness makes it impossible to use your natural talents and abilities, so that you never live up to your potential.

The second-worst danger from bipolar disorder is the loss of anything and everything you accomplished in your life. In bipolar episodes, people break up their families, destroy their marriages, and alienate their children, sometimes forever. I have watched many individuals destroy their careers, lose their homes and savings, and drive away their friends when their bipolar disorder was uncontrolled. I have seen people throw away fortunes, get pregnant, catch diseases, go to jail, and injure or kill themselves and others in accidents during bipolar episodes.

Are people with bipolar disorder more likely to kill themselves?

Suicide is a serious problem in this illness. Thirty percent of individuals with bipolar disorder will attempt suicide during their lives, and 20 percent will succeed. Even failed suicide attempts can cause crippling, lifelong injuries. Fortunately, your risk of suicide decreases dramatically when your bipolar disorder is treated.

Can I be hopeful about my future?

Absolutely. With successful treatment, people with bipolar disorder are healthy and can achieve the kind of life they want and deserve. For the first time in history, we have a broad choice of effective treatments for bipolar disorder, and there are even better, cutting-edge therapies about to be released (see chapter 3).

What can I do now to get my bipolar disorder under control?

Maintain your determination, find a good doctor, keep a healthy lifestyle, find medications that work, care for your psychological needs, and find strategies to do the things that bipolar disorder makes difficult. You can use this book to find how to do all these things and more.

Why do you think I need to learn about my bipolar disorder?

There is so little reliable information readily available about bipolar disorder that you, the patient, must become your own expert on your illness and your well-being. Once you have found a doctor and therapist who is/are knowledgeable about bipolar disorder, try to learn all you can. Ultimately, you must become the guiding force behind your own treatment, not through intuition or destiny, but by the knowledge of facts.

Why do you talk about bipolar disorder like it is a disease? I think I am a normal person.

In order to diagnose bipolar disorder, the symptoms must cause problems in major areas of your life such as work, school, social activities, and/or relationships with friends or family. Bipolar disorder is certainly a disease if it is keeping you from reaching your full potential in life.

However, if you bring your bipolar disorder under control with proper ongoing treatment, you can then use your full range of normal talents and abilities. At that point, in my opinion, you still have bipolar disorder, but it is not an illness.

CYCLING IN BIPOLAR DISORDER

Some but not all people with bipolar disorder experience a dramatic increase in symptoms at certain times of the year. These are called cycles. When the illness is young, cycles are more irregular, but as the disease matures, most individuals develop two to four episodes at about the same times every year. If the disease worsens, the number of episodes per year increases.

Q Someone told me I had "rapid cycling"
   bipolar disorder. What is that?

If you have more than four episodes of mania or depression in a year, you are said to suffer from rapid cycling. All the legitimate research that you will read about rapid cycling uses this definition.

Q I was told that I'm a rapid cycler because I
   have lots of angry episodes every day.
      Is this diagnosis correct?

When people have rapid emotional changes throughout the day, I call this emotional lability, not rapid cycling. Actually, sudden, brief outbursts of anger and/or depression are common in many mental and emotional situations. Having emotional lability does not prove that you have bipolar disorder.

Q Do people have symptoms between
   bipolar episodes?

Yes. Between episodes, people with bipolar illness often experience symptoms like persistent insomnia, anger, social anxiety, and struggles with communication and relationships. I often see patients that exhibit distractibility, difficulty staying on topic, and poor logical thought. There are sometimes illogical beliefs and obsessions that continue after the more obvious symptoms are gone. For example, a husband might become obsessively rageful after a minor disagreement with his wife and continue to hold a grudge for months, despite the pain it causes his family and the resultant deterioration of his marriage. These events are much less likely to occur when your illness is adequately treated.

Why do some people in online groups state that they are perfectly fine without treatment? They say I'm an idiot because I take medications.

I think that you are smart, not an idiot. I have investigated lots of claims of self-cures but I have never found one that was true. On the other hand, I have seen many people try to prove to themselves that they are fine by telling others that it is so. Lots of people with bipolar disorder have symptom-free periods, but without treatment, these periods never last.

I had a bipolar episode two months ago. Recently I stopped my medications and I'm fine now. Am I cured?

One of the unique features of bipolar disorder is that individuals may feel fine between their cycles. Everyone would like to believe that their illness has magically disappeared, but studies show that you are likely to relapse within two to three months after you stop your medications.

TIME COURSE

Untreated bipolar disorder usually grows worse with age. In uncontrolled bipolar disorder, the brain deteriorates in brain locations called the prefrontal and temporal areas, the amygdala, and the hippocampus.

How can I keep my bipolar disorder from growing worse as I age?

When bipolar episodes are controlled, I believe that worsening of the disease slows down or might even stop. The correct medications can stop bipolar episodes from happening, and some medications can even stimulate the brain to grow and repair brain cells.

I heard that bipolar disorder "burns out" and goes away when you get old. Is that true?

I have heard this story, too. However, when I examine people with "burned-out" bipolar disorder, I usually find burned-out elders who are so incapacitated with multiple health problems that their mental condition is the least of their worries.

How often does bipolar disorder go away on its own?

I have never known anyone whose bipolar symptoms went away without treatment.

CAUSES OF BIPOLAR DISORDER

Bipolar illness can be found in every nation and every culture from the beginning of written history. Contrary to past theories, bipolar disorder is not caused by hardship, poverty, or discrimination; it is not caused by poor education or poor parenting; and it is not a result of early childhood trauma or abuse. Stressful life events do not cause bipolar disorder, but the symptoms of bipolar illness do worsen in the presence of stress.

What causes bipolar disorder?

Bipolar disorder is caused by deficiencies in the physiology and biochemistry of the nervous system areas that control body, mind, and emotions. When someone has been bipolar for many years, the illness influences habits of thinking and behavior. This "excess baggage" is also an important part of bipolar disorder. One possible source of imbalance is too much reactivity of the natural stress response. Stress causes the release of natural neurochemicals and these neurochemicals worsen bipolar disorder.

What makes me feel like my body is sped up or slowed down?

Adrenaline is a natural substance that is released by the body during the stress response. If your adrenaline level was too high, you would feel many manic symptoms, such as speediness, hyperactivity, anxiety, and irritability. If your adrenaline was low, you would feel many symptoms of bipolar depression, such as fatigue, low motivation, and increased sleepiness. (Note that adrenaline is the commonly used name, but epinephrine and norepinephrine are the correct scientific names.)

Areas deep in the center of the brain called the hypothalamus–pituitary axis, or HP, help control the production of adrenaline. If the HP area is imbalanced, then adrenaline production can be too high, causing mania, or too low, causing depression. An imbalance in the HP area of the brain is one possible explanation for bipolar illness.

What makes my thinking change when my bipolar disorder acts up?

Bipolar disorder causes problems in keeping thoughts in or out of the conscious mind, a process I refer to as gating. Imagine that the conscious mind is a full house that can only hold five to nine thoughts at any one time. If the mind is occupied and the house is completely full, whenever the gate lets in an unwanted thought it pushes one of the existing thoughts out of the gate and that thought is lost. Under these conditions, it becomes difficult to keep unwanted thoughts out or hold relevant thoughts in the conscious mind. You can see that this gating problem makes people with bipolar disorder very vulnerable to distractions, strong emotions, and obsessive thinking. Over time, this deficit can lead to memory problems, difficulty concentrating, difficulty following conversations, a tendency to interrupt others when they are speaking, and a tendency to deviate from the point of conversation.

Is bipolar disorder inherited?

Bipolar disorder is more likely to occur in children of bipolar parents. Research studies show that if your mother or father has bipolar disorder then you are seven times more likely to have the illness than the average population. If your brother or sister has bipolar disorder, then your risk of getting it increases to fifteen times the average population. If you have an identical twin who is bipolar, your risk increases to sixty-five times the population average.

Do certain genes carry the bipolar disease from parent to child?

When scientists compare the DNA of individuals with bipolar disorder with the DNA from their family members who do not have the disease, they find that certain genes are associated with bipolar disorder. Some of the bipolar genes are named 4p, 18p11, 11q2-23, and 22q.

Scientists do not know the exact way that genes cause bipolar disorder, but we can theorize. We know that the release of too much adrenaline into the blood can mimic manic symptoms, and too little adrenaline released into the blood can mimic depressive symptoms. Your DNA can produce three similar forms of switches that affect adrenaline response, called receptors alpha-2A, alpha-2B, and alpha-2C. If your DNA produces more alpha-2A switches, then more adrenaline might be turned on to increase manic symptoms. However, if your DNA produces more of the other switches, your adrenaline response will be reduced and you may experience depressed symptoms. Similarly, a common mutation in the receptor DNA (serine at position 201) can stop nerves from releasing certain adrenaline-like compounds, possibly creating depressed symptoms. These are examples of how changes at the DNA level might affect the function of your brain and nervous system.

What other areas of the brain might cause bipolar disorder?

Experts suspect that bipolar disorder is active in several interconnected brain areas, called the amygdala, frontal lobe, temporal lobe, and the hippocampus. Studies show that brain cells in these areas die at a more rapid rate in individuals with bipolar disorder. We also know that injury, strokes, or epilepsy in the temporal lobe can cause symptoms that resemble bipolar disorder. When I have tested individuals hours to days after their first bipolar episode, I have found cognitive problems associated with the temporal lobe area. This would also help explain why most of the mood stabilizers that block bipolar disorder can also be used to block temporal lobe epilepsy.

Having a manic or depressed episode may also cause permanent changes in the brain cells of the amygdala, so that it is easier for these cells to fire abnormally. This phenomenon is called potentiation. After the response of these cells is altered, the potentiation can then spread to other parts of the brain. This is one explanation of why uncontrolled manic episodes appear to make bipolar disorder irreversibly worse.

Are mania and bipolar depression different disorders?

It is a mistake to view mania and depression as if they were two separate disorders. It is the underlying bipolar disease that causes both mania and bipolar depression. Therefore, it is important that bipolar flare-ups are treated with mood stabilizers, whether they are mainly manic or mainly depressive in nature.

Are mania and bipolar depression like two poles with normal in the middle?

I do not believe that bipolar disorder is like a line with mania on one end, depression on the other, and normalcy in between. It is an important issue, because if doctors follow this model, they may try to treat bipolar depressed symptoms by giving inappropriate medications "to make the person a little more manic." In my experience, this only worsens the disorder.

Instead, I see bipolar disorder like a hairpin, with normalcy on one end and both mania and depression on the other. This is the only way to explain why both manic and depressed symptoms are often seen at the same time. Moreover, when someone switches from extreme mania, they go directly to extreme depression; they do not go through normal on the way from one to the other. This is why treating the underlying bipolar imbalance with medications specifically used for bipolar disorder helps reduce mania and keep depressive episodes from happening in the first place. See chapter 3 for more details on medication treatment options.

BIPOLAR MANIA

Mania refers to the mental, emotional, and physical experiences that comprise the activated stage of bipolar disorder. These symptoms are called manic symptoms, and when they predominate, the condition is called a manic episode. When manic symptoms are seen in the presence of depressed symptoms, the condition is called a mixed episode.

What is the official definition of mania? What are true manic symptoms?

The official definition of a manic episode used in the United States is found in the American Psychiatric Association's *Diagnostic and Statistical Manual of Mental Disorders, Fourth Edition (DSM-IV-TR)*; see appendix A for the official wording. (The National Institute of Mental Health has published a useful alternative list of combined symptoms of mania that may be found in appendix B.) I have adapted the DSM definition of mania for my patients as follows:

A. A distinct period of abnormally and persistently irritable, elevated, and/or expansive mood, lasting at least one week, AND:

B. During this period, three or more of the following symptoms (or four if mood is only irritable) have persisted and have been present to a significant degree:

1. Has a decreased need for sleep (for example, sleeps only three hours per night)
2. Is very talkative (may interrupt or finish others' sentences and/or has difficulty stopping the flow of speech)
3. Has rapid thoughts (a feeling that thoughts are racing)
4. Is very distractible (distractibility can also affect attention and/or memory)
5. Is overfocused on work, school, personal or sexual activities, and/or has a feeling of physical edginess or agitation
6. Takes risky chances such as reckless driving, overspending, sexual indiscretions, or entering risky business schemes
7. Has an inflated sense of self-esteem

C. The symptoms cause problems in major areas of life such as work, school, social activities, and/or relationships with friends or family.

It is very important to note that the dominant emotion in mania can be (and often is) irritability and anger. Many cases of mania are misdiagnosed because of the expectation that the patient's mood will be elated. To have mania you do not need to be smiling, laughing, happy, high, elated, or show any other elevated emotion. The most common symptoms that I see in my patients are angry mood, rapid speech, and distractibility. Also, note that manic symptoms are usually in the normal range of behaviors but are extreme or exaggerated.

Mania makes my spouse turn into a different person. Is this multiple personalities?

Not necessarily. Mania can change individuals so much that they act like different people. However, as you can see from the list above, mania can produce changes in attention, activity, mood, thoughts, and attitude. These do not represent different personalities. They are all aspects of bipolar disorder.

Supposedly, manics can't sleep, but I can't even wake up in the morning. How can I be manic?

In severe mania, little or no sleep is possible throughout the day or night. In less severe circumstances, the most common bipolar sleep pattern is to stay up at night and be sleepy during the day.

I stay up until 3:00 A.M. every night. Aren't I a normal night person?

No single criterion can make the diagnosis of bipolar disorder. Many people feel better late at night and describe themselves simply as "night people." However, if you stay up all night and also match enough of the diagnostic criteria for mania, then you are a night person *with mania*.

My son-in-law talks a mile a minute. Is he manic?

When someone speaks too rapidly, the usual explanation you will hear is that it is cultural, regional, or familial. However, rapid, pressured speech can also be an indication of mania.

Sometimes I think so fast that my mouth can't keep up with my thoughts. Could this be like mania?

Thoughts that go by so fast that you cannot follow them are called racing thoughts. When your speech tries to follow your thoughts, plunging ahead despite other people's attempts to speak, it is called pressured speech. These thought patterns are characteristic of mania.

My doctor muttered something about how
   I was "tangential." What does she
   mean by that?

In mania, speech can flow from your mouth in a never-ending torrent. This, coupled with distractibility, can cause you to stray from the point (tangential speech) or lose the point entirely (blocking). If you add too many unnecessary details, side remarks, and lengthy buildups to your conversation, it is called circumstantial speech.

I'm told that that I smile and laugh too
   much, even when I'm talking about
   something sad. Is this a symptom
   of bipolar disorder?

Although it is not one of the diagnostic criteria, people with bipolar disorder frequently smile, giggle, and laugh without appearing to notice. When the topic is serious or sad, this smiling and laughing can appear quite odd to others. We call this inappropriate affect. When I notice this, I help patients become more aware of their expressions, so they can be more successful in their communication.

Why do I have so many thoughts? They
   distract me during the day and they keep
   me from falling asleep at night.

Intrusive thoughts are a primary component of bipolar disorder. During the day, many people learn to mask these thoughts by distracting themselves with work and other activities, but at night when you are trying to go to sleep, the thoughts come back full force and keep you awake.

Are attention problems and distractibility
 prominent symptoms of mania?

Unless adequately treated, every person with bipolar disorder has some attention problems, usually arising from distractibility. To the trained eye, distractibility shows itself as lapses in conversation, getting off track, and being
interrupted by external or internal stimuli. Distractibility can be measured
by a neuropsych examination using tests such as the Connor's CPT or the
Gordon test of attention. In these tests, you sit behind a computer or a console that provides stimuli at different speeds and combinations. Then a soft-
ware program evaluates how distractible you are. These tests are often
available in hospitals, testing centers, or in the offices of medical specialists
and psychologists.

My memory is awful. Could this be due
 to my bipolar disorder?

Bipolar distractibility can interfere with the flow of information into your
brain and lead to poor memory. In particular, there is a tendency to forget
names, numbers, dates, times, amounts, distances, and similar details.

What is wrong with being manic? Last time
 I was manic I completely cleaned
 up my apartment.

I call this the "kitchen sink phenomenon." Whenever I hear that someone
stopped their medication and became so energized that they went home
and started cleaning out the area under their kitchen sink, I look to see if
mania is present. Taking on large projects like suddenly beginning to paint
the house is another clue. Unfortunately, these heroic projects are often left
unfinished. Ultimately, mania causes more harm than good, especially when
it is followed by bipolar depression.

I have to stay manic so I can get everything done. I *have* to be productive.

That is the kind of thought distortion that characterizes mania. Remember that your first duty to yourself is to protect your own health; it is a basic component of self-respect. You need to see your doctor and find out the best things to do to end this manic episode. Later on, when your thoughts are clear, I expect that you will see things differently. Only then will you be able to use your talents and abilities to their best advantage.

I spend all my time obsessing about famous people and sex. Am I losing my mind?

Associating oneself with people who are famous, powerful, and/or sexually attractive can feed the need to feel special and to look special in the eyes of others. Although it is not part of the diagnostic criteria, many manics show this preoccupation with celebrity and are powerless to stop these intrusive thoughts. However, there are medications that can return control of your thoughts to you.

Why do I feel obsessed with someone I met only once, many years ago?

I have often seen obsessions, infatuations, and sexual attraction to unlikely persons in mania. Sometimes obsessions suddenly develop about friends, neighbors, and acquaintances who never seemed important before. These feelings usually fade after the mania is brought under control.

Periodically I go out and spend way too much money. Is this mania?

Mania often produces spending sprees. I always ask my patients if they have clothes or shoes in their closet that have never been worn or still have their price tags. I remember a patient who arrived in my office late and quite manic. "On the way over here," he told me, "I stopped off in a store and bought a ten-thousand-dollar computer. The funniest thing is that I do not even know how to work a computer." Because insight is impaired by mania, these behaviors seem perfectly reasonable during the manic episode, making spending sprees difficult to combat.

The criteria for mania mentions poor judgment. Can you give an example?

I once worked with a bipolar woman who put the fate of her successful company in the hands of her secretary. She gave him keys to the office, account numbers, passwords, and complete access to all the business's money. One day this woman came to my office crushed because the secretary had withdrawn all her money, sold her equipment, and skipped town. My patient worked hard to salvage her business, but, to my surprise, in six months the same secretary was back with the same responsibilities as before. My patient's reasoning was this: "I can't see how he would have the nerve to steal from me again." None of this would have happened if my patient had been able to exercise her natural good judgment, which had become clouded by bipolar disorder.

Do wild manic schemes ever work?

Mania often leads people to start businesses, investments, or moneymaking schemes that show poor judgment. However, there is always an exception to the rule. I knew two people who had manic business ideas at the same time. One started an after-school babysitting service. She continued to work on her business idea for years after her bipolar disorder was well controlled, and it prospered. The other person sank his money into a scheme to buy jewelry from television shopping channels and sell it through newspaper classified advertisements. This idea was a financial disaster. The moral is that dramatic ideas conceived during mania sometimes work out, but only if you get healthy and work on them.

What is grandiosity?

Some people with bipolar disorder so crave the admiration and approval of others that they misrepresent themselves. In the simplest form, they may act important and imagine that they deserve special recognition and considerations. They may tell exaggerated stories about themselves or imply that they possess wealth, power, influential friends, mystical abilities, or special spiritual standing. When the illness is severe, people with bipolar disorder may even believe these lies themselves. These behaviors are driven by internal feelings of omnipotence, the belief that rules and social conventions do not apply to them, and the sense that they are better than other people.

My family doctor told me that I couldn't have bipolar disorder because I don't act "crazy." I had a similar experience with a therapist friend. What do professionals expect to see when a manic patient comes to them?

The first person I ever saw with bipolar disorder was the stereotype of mania. He arrived at the hospital in a white stretch limousine and stepped out wearing a bright white three-piece linen suit, a white snap-brim fedora hat, white patent leather shoes, and a black silk dress shirt with a white silk tie. He swaggered up the walkway, beaming at the passersby, as if he were the director of the hospital. As he walked past a courtyard basketball game, he stepped out, caught the ball, and shot a perfect basket across the court. He was so dramatic and so magnetic that he looked like he had stepped out of the Academy Awards ceremony. He stepped through the hospital door, made a grand bow to the staff, and shouted, "I'm here! And I'm *manic*!"

After seeing this, I was sure that I would never have any trouble recognizing mania. Fortunately, a brilliant clinician named Dr. Margarita Lermo leaned over and whispered to me, "This is what everyone expects a manic to look like. However, the bipolar patients in your private practice will look just like everyone else." Just as she predicted, although I can usually recognize mania in my patients, they usually look fine to others without special training. This is why well-meaning professionals may tell you, "Oh, no! You can't be manic!"

My brother told me that his depression was caused by his mania. Is this on the level?

A lifetime ago, many analysts believed that mania was caused by a reaction to the intolerable experience of depression. Nowadays, most doctors believe that mania usually precedes depression. It seems reasonable to me that, as the natural manic episode draws to a close, the sheer fatigue and exhaustion of mania helps precipitate a crash into the deactivated state of bipolar depression.

BIPOLAR DEPRESSION

Bipolar depression is an inactivated state where people suffer from low motivation, low energy, good appetite, frequent weight gain, and daytime sleepiness. They often cannot get out of bed and they may say, "I just can't function." We have known about the specific features of bipolar depression since the 1800s, although the names have changed. For example, earlier in history bipolar depression symptoms were called hysteroid dysphoria and neurasthenia. Even the term "depression" is probably a bad choice of words because it suggests that unipolar major depression and bipolar depression are similar. However, these are different diseases, located in different parts of the brain and driven by different biochemical systems.

Is bipolar disorder mainly mania or mainly depression?

Bipolar disorder is mainly depression. Almost 70 percent of all those with bipolar disorder are depressed at any one time. People who cycle spend three times as much time being depressed as being manic. When bipolar disorder is insufficiently treated, people spend an average of four months of the year in depression. Furthermore, depression seems to increase with age.

Many individuals experience mainly manic symptoms during their youth, but as they grow older their disease manifests itself as depression.

How is bipolar depression diagnosed?

Some doctors prefer to rely on establishing a past history of cycling episodes to make the diagnosis of bipolar depression. A few doctors still believe that bipolar and unipolar depression are the same illness. However, I believe that bipolar depression is so distinctive that it usually can be differentiated from other types of depression by direct examination.

At the present time, there is no listing for "bipolar depression" in the official manual of medical diagnoses. "Physical slowing with or without oversleeping" is the way one major authority (*Kaplan & Sadock's Comprehensive Textbook of Psychiatry*; see chapter 10) characterizes bipolar depression.

From my years of observing and treating bipolar patients, I believe that the diagnosis psychiatrists know as "atypical depression" is most like bipolar depression. However, not all professionals agree with me (yet). The official definition of atypical depression is found in the American Psychiatric Association's *Diagnostic and Statistical Manual of Mental Disorders, Fourth Edition* (*DSM-IV-TR*) found in appendix A. I have adapted this definition of atypical (bipolar) depression for my patients as follows:

A. A period lasting two weeks or more where the mood is depressed most of the day nearly every day, OR
there is markedly diminished interest or pleasure in almost all activities.
B. The mood can brighten with good news (even if it is only for minutes or hours) AND:
C. At least two of the following:
1. An increase in weight and/or appetite.
2. A tendency to sleep too much during the day (called hypersomnia).
3. A feeling of fatigue and/or paralysis such that it feels impossible to perform daily activities.
4. A long-standing pattern of easily hurt feelings.
D. The symptoms cause problems in major areas of life such as work, school, social activities, and/or relationships with friends or family.

Other features that I often see in bipolar depression include agitation, anxiety, social withdrawal, distractibility, procrastination, the inability to start or finish projects, memory problems, and deteriorating self-care. The National Institute of Mental Health has published a list of combined symptoms of both bipolar depression and unipolar major depression that you may find in appendix B.

How is bipolar depression different from common unipolar major depression?

The most frequent symptoms of bipolar depression are daytime sleepiness, weight gain, fatigue, low motivation, and easily hurt feelings. In contrast, people with unipolar major depression usually experience early waking, inability to get back to sleep in the morning, weight loss, and constant thoughts of death.

Are people with bipolar depression overweight? I eat nothing, but I'm still gaining weight.

Many of my depressed bipolar patients have gained weight even when they said they were on austere diets. Low activity, low metabolism, and increased appetite can all conspire to increase weight gain during bipolar depression.

I have bipolar depression, and I can't stop bingeing on chocolate and carbohydrates! Do I have an eating disorder?

You certainly have a problem with your eating, but it is a part of your bipolar disorder and not a separate diagnosis. A variety of eating problems are seen in the context of bipolar depression. For example, early psychiatrists noted chocolate craving in what we now know as bipolar depression. In my experience, this usually takes the form of eating chocolate ice cream. We will explore dietary issues in more detail in chapter 2.

Do people with bipolar depression sleep all day and night?

Most bipolar depressed people start out by staying up late at night and feel-ing sleepy during the day. Then they may progress to where they cannot get up in the morning at all.

I spend all day in a daze, daydreaming. Have you heard of this before?

There is a dramatic, biochemically driven change in brain function during bipolar depression. During the day, if they are not sleeping, people with bipolar depression often spend their time lying on the couch or bed in a daze, dozing or daydreaming. Some people remember the daydreams and multiple thoughts. Others cannot remember that they were thinking any-thing or may just experience a gap in their memory.

I'm a real procrastinator. Is that related to bipolar depression?

The tendency to put things off until the last minute is very common in bipolar depression. It is as if your motivation is so low that only the danger of failure can force you to finish your project.

Am I lazy? I can't get up to go to work, and I seem to lie around all day.

No. Your bipolar depression is not laziness. It is a nervous system disease that turns off your ability to stay active, no matter how hard you try. This issue often comes up when families, friends, and employers see individuals with bipolar disorder. Because they do not know about bipolar illness, they may assume that the individual is just lazy.

When I get depressed, I stay inside and I never answer my telephone or mail. Could I have bipolar depression?

I frequently see bipolar depression causing social isolation, withdrawal, and an inability to keep up communications with others. When this is severe, it may resemble the diagnosis of agoraphobia, although agoraphobia does not come with a history of bipolar symptoms. This kind of avoidance can torpedo friendships, family relations, and employment, but, fortunately, the withdrawal gradually fades with effective bipolar treatment.

I feel paralyzed. Why can't I do anything?

You are describing a state that is specific and understandable to you and others with bipolar depression but has little meaning for the general public. People with bipolar depression use words like "being paralyzed," "being overwhelmed," "unable to function," and "unable to do anything."

This condition is a major cause of problems in bipolar depression. It may involve the brain centers that control conscious movement and activity, such as the *substantia nigra* area of the brain. For example, insufficient quantities of the biochemical dopamine, an important neurotransmitter in bipolar disorder, in the *substantia nigra* cause an inability to move and initiate actions in Parkinson's disorder. Happily, this paralyzed state usually improves significantly in both disorders with appropriate treatment.

What does bipolar depression feel like?

Many people associate the term depression with feelings of sadness, and sadness is indeed what most persons with unipolar major depression feel. However, by questioning my patients with bipolar depression, I have learned that, unlike those with unipolar depression, they experience a mixture of emotions, including sadness, hopelessness, anxiety, panic, fear, irritability, and anger, which are often difficult to distinguish from one another.

Bipolar depression brings with it an intense internal pain so strong that individuals often spend entire days crying. Many feel as though they are immobilized and that they can never reach the goals they have set for themselves.

But isn't depression the same in everyone?

Not necessarily. For one thing, depression feels different in the two disorders. For example, I once interviewed a therapist who had come for help with unipolar major depression:

W.B.: How do you feel?

Pt: I feel depressed. You know what that's like: I feel sad.

W.B.: Do you feel anxious?

Pt: No, I feel sad.

W.B.: Well, do you feel panicky?

Pt: No, I only feel sad.

W.B.: What about irritability?

Pt: (now *becoming* irritated) No, I'm depressed, you idiot! All I feel is sad, sad, sad! Nothing else.

In contrast, persons with bipolar depression usually feel a mix of anxiety, panic, pessimism, irritability, etc. When I tell this story to persons with bipolar depression, they are surprised at the difference between how they feel and how this patient with unipolar major depression felt.

But I'm anxious *and* depressed. What is going on?

Based on my experience, I believe that many people who used to be diagnosed with "anxious depression" really had bipolar depression. Bipolar disorder makes worried thoughts by producing repetitive and intrusive thinking and by overfocusing attention on what will happen in the future. Physical edginess and agitation are also caused by bipolar disorder. Persons with bipolar disorder describe this feeling as "on edge," "like my body isn't right," "like I'm jumping out of my skin," etc.

Why am I so angry at myself?
    I haven't done anything wrong.

Bipolar disorder by itself makes you feel depressed, anxious, angry, or dulled. It causes depression by altering the parts of your body chemistry that control emotions. However, when bipolar disorder makes us feel bad we do not initially realize that this is a body response to the disease. Instead, we attempt to find some intellectual reason for our depression and end up criticizing ourselves for no good reason.

It is hard to hear encouragement when you are depressed, but please try to understand that you have not done anything wrong. You are only experiencing the physical effects of an illness that targets our emotions, among other things.

How does the rate of suicide in bipolar
    depression compare to other
    emotional disorders?

Suicide is more common in bipolar depression than in unipolar major depression, panic disorder, or even schizophrenia. However, the suicide rate goes down dramatically with adequate treatment.

My doctor diagnosed me with "treatment
    resistant depression" because nothing
    that I have taken works. Could I really
    have bipolar depression?

It is sometimes very hard to distinguish unipolar major depression from bipolar depression. I am frequently asked to see "treatment resistant" depressed individuals who have been given many antidepressants without any effect. Many of these people turn out to have unrecognized bipolar depression. When they are given the mood stabilizers that are used to treat bipolar disorder, their depression lifts. If this sounds like you, discuss it with your doctor and/or consider seeking a second opinion.

Is depression hard to treat in bipolar disorder?

By the time mania has triggered a depressive episode, it may already be hard to treat. In this case, psychotherapy and medical treatment are aimed at relieving symptoms until the depressive episode goes away. Ultimately, the real treatment for bipolar depression is to find the right medications that prevent manic or depressive episodes from starting in the first place.

BIPOLAR TYPES I, II, AND III

Doctors have created a classification system of "types" for bipolar disorder in an attempt to distinguish between people with varying symptoms. Type I describes those who have clear manic and depressed cycles. Type II describes those individuals whose cycles are unequal and have, for example, mainly depressed symptoms most of the time with only occasional manic symptoms. Type III is an unofficial category applied to people with bipolar disorder whose first episode is triggered by an antidepressant medication.

Part of the reason for these extra categories is to overcome the traditional misconception that bipolar disorder always manifests as a cyclic disorder with clear episodes of pure mania and pure depression. While these categories help clear up some of the uncertainty about bipolar disorder, there is still a great amount of confusion in the research and literature about bipolar disorder. One reason is that many people who have personality disorders or organic brain injury are now included in the Bipolar Type II category, although they do not really have bipolar disorder.

I have depression, not bipolar disorder! I am depressed most of the time, and I have never had a mood elevation in my life.

Even if you only experience depression, you still might have bipolar disorder Type II. Remember that you do not have to experience mood elevation to have mania. Many manics experience irritable (angry) or expansive or mixed moods rather than elation.

Is treatment less effective for Type II bipolar disorder than Type I?

Some studies suggest so. However, the present population of Type II patients in research studies contains a mixture of individuals with different neuropsychiatric problems other than bipolar disorder, so it is difficult to interpret studies comparing Types I and II.

MIXED-STATE BIPOLAR DISORDER

The presence of manic and depressed symptoms together is called mixed-state bipolar disorder. If you experience this, you are not alone. Many bipolar individuals experience the same thing.

How common is the "mixed" type of bipolar disorder?

A recent study showed that 13 percent of bipolar patients had mixed symptoms. However, this does not fit with my clinical observations. After I have time to examine and get to know my patients I have found that almost everyone with bipolar disorder has a mixture of some manic and some depressed symptoms.

GETTING THE RIGHT DIAGNOSIS

A clinician friend once told me with disdain, "*I* don't concern myself with *diagnoses.*" Another asked me, "Why do you have to remind people that they have problems? Can't you just ignore people's differences?"

It would be nice if we could make bipolar disorder go away by ignoring it. However, you will soon see that accurate diagnosis is the most important tool to keep you healthy in bipolar disorder. Getting the correct diagnosis can make the difference between getting successful treatment or dragging along for years without being able to use your unique skills and talents. Correct diagnosis can help avoid erroneous and dangerous treatments. The ability to detect when bipolar illness is worsening can help head off flare-ups before they start.

What would I see if my loved one had bipolar disorder?

During an activated or manic episode, some of the following symptoms will be present:

- Talking abnormally loudly and rapidly and/or talking too much
- Staying up all night
- Starting new projects that are never finished and making unplanned trips
- Racing thoughts and a feeling that the mind is too full of thoughts, especially at bedtime
- Making impulsive decisions and becoming obsessed about work or re-lationships
- Exhibiting sudden changes in dress and grooming, particularly at the beginning of an episode
- Taking risks (such as driving too fast) or other deviations from usual behavior

During an inactivated or depressed episode, some of the following symptoms will be present:

- Oversleeping
- Overeating and/or gaining weight
- Tiredness and low motivation that make it difficult to start or finish even simple tasks
- Withdrawing from social situations by avoiding telephone calls and mail or remaining in one's room or home

How can I tell for sure if I have bipolar disorder?

Find a doctor experienced with bipolar disorder who will give you a professional evaluation to determine if bipolar disorder is present and what you should do about it. You can ask for a referral from a family physician or therapist or go directly to a medical specialist (psychiatrist). For more information about how and where to get help, see chapter 4 and chapter 10.

What should I do if I suspect that someone I care about has bipolar disorder?

All you can do is to help them get specialized professional help. You are not trained as a specialist in bipolar disorder and you should not try to take over this role. It may damage your relationship with this person if you try.

How can I tell if a doctor is taking my illness seriously?

You want your doctor to work seriously on determining this diagnosis because it is one of the most important things you will ever do in your life. Try to find a doctor who will spend at least thirty to sixty minutes of serious evaluation before she or he offers a diagnosis. Sometimes you may have to visit the doctor two or more times until a diagnosis can be made. At the end of the evaluation, ask your doctor to explain exactly what your diagnosis is and on what the diagnostic decision has been based.

What do you do in an evaluation?

Generally, I start out with thirty minutes of testing and self-rating paperwork that allows the prospective patient to record her or his own personal experiences. Then I sit and talk with them, asking them about the history of their problems and what has made their symptoms better or worse. I try to get to know who they are, how they think and feel, and what kind of life they want to have. I discuss what they have written down for me, and I may request additional medical tests or examinations. Finally, I discuss my conclusions or, if I still need more information, I ask them to return for a second appointment for more of the same.

Do doctors use written tests? What do you do?

It varies between doctors. I have patients make a simple family tree of mental, emotional, and social problems among their family members. I ask them to rate themselves on the formal diagnostic criteria of the American Psychiatric Association's *Diagnostic and Statistical Manual* (see appendix A). I administer clinical tests of depression, anxiety, obsessive and psychotic thought processes, and symptom severity, as well as personality tests. I may ask them to take tests I have written and published and/or perform neuropsych testing.

Will I get a physical examination?

Some psychiatrists will perform their own physical examination, but others (including myself) prefer to have the results of a physical examination made by your family physician. If there are any abnormalities in the results or more evaluation is needed, you may be referred to a specialist.

Will I get blood tests?

Often blood tests are drawn as part of a patient's regular checkup. Your doctor may want to get a blood cell count and/or tests of the kidneys, liver, thyroid, or other organs to rule out other diseases that imitate or worsen bipolar disorder.

Q How can you be certain of a bipolar
      diagnosis? Isn't bipolar disorder different
      in every person?

People are different but the disease is the same. For example, if you had a
party of one hundred completely different people who all had bipolar disorder, you could walk through the group and hear everyone saying similar
things about their bipolar illness, sometimes using the same words.

Q Where else can I find out information
      on bipolar disorder?

Go out and join national organizations representing bipolar disorder, get
and read professionally published magazines and newsletters, and go to national and local meetings of bipolar and mental health associations. Resources, in chapter 10, will get you started.

MISDIAGNOSIS

A recent study showed that almost 70 percent of bipolar patients had
been misdiagnosed more than three times before receiving their correct diagnosis. Common misdiagnoses include unipolar depression, attention deficit
disorder, sleep disorders, personality disorders, obsessive-compulsive disorder, post-traumatic stress disorder, postpartum depression, schizophrenia,
"stress," "nerves," and "old age."

Q A doctor told me I couldn't possibly have
　　bipolar disorder because I hadn't had a
　　manic episode, and diagnosed me with
　　unipolar depression. Then I had one.
　　Does this mean I am bipolar?

Yes, your bipolar disorder was mistaken for unipolar major depression. Misdiagnosing bipolar depression as unipolar major depression is the biggest mistake made in diagnosing bipolar disorder. Some studies suggest that more than half of the people with bipolar depression were previously misdiagnosed as having unipolar major depression.

One of the most unfortunate results of this misdiagnosis is that people with bipolar depression may receive antidepressant medications (like Prozac, Zoloft, or Celexa) that can worsen their bipolar depression and trigger mania and psychosis that can tear apart their careers and families. Antidepressants can even make bipolar illness *irreversibly* more severe for the rest of their life. This is one reason why doctors cannot try "treating for unipolar major depression first, just to see."

Q I have poor attention. Doesn't that mean
　　I have ADHD, not bipolar disorder?

Attention deficit hyperactivity disorder (ADHD) is a condition of poor focus and impulsive behavior that occurs in both children and adults. However, poor attention is also almost always seen in bipolar disorder as a result of the distractibility that is part of the disease.

Bipolar disorder is often misdiagnosed as ADHD. In fact, one study showed that out of a large sample of children diagnosed with ADHD, more than 25 percent really had bipolar disorder. Popular books often confuse the issue by describing both illnesses vaguely and by making ADHD seem more prevalent than it really is. As a result of misdiagnosis, many people with bipolar disorder are given medications that could make their condition worse.

I seem to match your criteria for bipolar
    disorder, but I've been diagnosed with
    a sleep disorder. Which is it?

Almost all of the people I have treated for bipolar disorder have had sleep problems, either from insufficient sleep or from oversleeping. Some people who are being treated for persistent, long-term insomnia may actually have undiagnosed bipolar disorder. However, bipolar disorder is not widely recognized by sleep disorder specialists as a potential cause for sleep disturbances. That is why it is so important for you to find a physician who is aware of the potential symptoms of bipolar disorder and who can give a well-informed assessment and diagnosis.

Bipolar depression causes symptoms of daytime sleepiness and fatigue, the urge to take daytime naps, and difficulty getting up in the morning. If your sleep problems are due to bipolar disorder, they will get better when the bipolar disorder is treated. Ask your sleep doctor and your psychiatrist to talk together to help resolve this situation.

Why did the emergency room doctor say
    I had panic disorder if I really have
    bipolar disorder?

Bipolar disorder causes a very high adrenaline drive that can appear to be due to panic disorder or other hyperactive states. Misdiagnosis is common, especially if you are seeing a new doctor who doesn't have access to your past medical records. People with true panic disorder do not have a history of other bipolar symptoms.

If you experience panic, worried thoughts, fears, and agitation, I suggest you strengthen the treatment for your bipolar disorder rather than treat your immediate panic symptoms. The sedatives and antidepressants used to treat the illness of panic disorder may provide only brief relief or they may make your anxiety symptoms worse.

What is hyperventilation? Does it have anything to do with the panic I feel?

When you or people you know complain of panic, ask if they have numbness or "pins and needles" (paresthesias) around their mouth, face, fingers, and/or toes. These are often signs of hyperventilation. In hyperventilation, people breathe too fast and change the acid/base balance in their brain. Difficulty getting one's breath, dizziness, and the feeling that one is going to black out often accompany hyperventilation. Hyperventilation is commonly mistaken for panic, and it can be relieved by making a conscious effort to breathe more slowly.

I heard there is something called generalized anxiety disorder, which seems to match my symptoms exactly. I went to another doctor and she agreed. Could this be mistaken for bipolar disorder?

Most people with bipolar disorder have symptoms of *generalized anxiety disorder* (GAD), including restlessness, edginess, easy fatigability, difficulty concentrating, irritability, muscle tension, and sleep disturbance. These symptoms are similar to what happens when adrenaline levels are high. However, people suffering from GAD do not have the other symptoms of bipolar disorder that are described in chapter 1.

When a noted research physician advertised for patients with generalized anxiety disorder for his research, he complained to me that "A significant proportion of them turned out to have bipolar disorder instead of GAD." My patients could have told him that.

I've started to obsess about things. Could my bipolar disorder have changed to obsessive-compulsive disorder (OCD)?

Probably not. Obsessive and compulsive symptoms are common in bipolar disorder. Intrusive and repeating thoughts are a key component of bipolar disorder. Persons with bipolar disorder are also vulnerable to some obsessive behaviors, such as counting stones in the sidewalk or stairs in a building. Conversely, true OCD does not come with a history of bipolar symptoms (see chapter 1).

If you have bipolar disorder, work on strengthening your bipolar treatment and your obsessions and compulsions are likely to wane. Some psychotherapy and medication treatments used in OCD (such as antidepressants) can make bipolar disorder worse. I know a woman whose bipolar disorder had been treated well for twenty years with mood stabilizers. Unfortunately, when she saw a new young student doctor, he observed her obsessiveness and changed her diagnosis from bipolar disorder to OCD. Her medications were also changed, which ultimately made her have violent hallucinations of war and bloody carnage. This resolved when she was put back on her former medication.

Why was my brother initially misdiagnosed with schizophrenia and then later diagnosed with bipolar disorder?

Although hallucinations, delusions, and flattened emotions can be caused by severe bipolar disorder as well as schizophrenia, many people with these symptoms are simply dropped into the category of schizophrenia. Over the years, almost a quarter of the patients I have seen with diagnoses of chronic schizophrenia had undiagnosed bipolar disorder. I have seen many people in institutions with "untreatable schizophrenia" bounce back after they were given an adequate trial of mood stabilizers.

Q I thought I had bipolar disorder but my other doctor said I probably just had thyroid problems. Does low or high thyroid create symptoms like those of bipolar disorder?

Persons with bipolar disorder can have thyroid problems, too. Moreover, all doctors are taught in medical school that insufficient thyroid hormones (hypothyroidism) looks like clinical depression and overabundant thyroid hormones (hyperthyroidism) looks like mania. Ask your psychiatrist and your other doctor to talk together.

Q My wife won't leave the house. Could she be bipolar *and* agoraphobic?

Agoraphobia refers to the condition where people refuse to leave their house and/or room. However, feelings of withdrawal and the need for isolation are also familiar to people with bipolar depression. The distinguishing difference is that true agoraphobia does not come with the other history and symptoms of bipolar disorder that I have already outlined. The most severe cases of agoraphobia I have treated turned out to be caused by severe bipolar depression. These individuals had paranoia and a fear of being around and interacting with other people. Often these poor individuals had spent much of their life in their bed or on the couch.

Medications including antidepressants that are prescribed for agoraphobia could make bipolar disorder worse. If your wife has been diagnosed with agoraphobia but also exhibits symptoms of bipolar disorder, then she should consult a psychiatrist that specializes in bipolar disorder to determine if she has been given the correct diagnosis.

I think my symptoms are more consistent
    with fibromyalgia, and my
    neurologist agrees.

People can have both disorders, and some of the symptoms of fibromyalgia overlap with those of bipolar depression. If bipolar depression is one possibility, ask your neurologist if she or he would consider a trial of a mood stabilizer and see if your symptoms improve.

I'm sure I have chronic fatigue syndrome (CFS).
    Why should I take a mood stabilizer?

The severe fatigue present in bipolar depression can be mistaken for CFS. If your doctor suggests a mood stabilizer, you should consider trying it. Feeling better is what really matters.

I don't think I have bipolar disorder. I think
    I'm reacting to natural events that
    happen to me. I can find a cause for
    every symptom on your list.

Of course you can. Stress from the environment affects everyone, especially persons with bipolar disorder. An important goal of bipolar treatment is to make you less vulnerable to these outside stressors.

What's the most common problem that's
    misdiagnosed as severe bipolar disorder?

Drug abuse. High doses of methamphetamine, cocaine, and/or PCP can create behavior that looks very much like mania. When I worked in an emergency room, I once treated a basketball player who was intoxicated with PCP. He was hyperactive, talked a mile a minute, and looked very manic at that time. At one point in my interview he jumped straight in the air, broke through the suspended ceiling, and proceeded to crawl around above everyone else's heads for hours before we could get him to come down. However, he did not have bipolar disorder. When he woke in the morning, he was back to his usual self, and I sent him home.

I'm thirty years old, and I was just diagnosed with bipolar disorder. Why did it take so long?

There are many possible reasons why it can take a long time for your bipolar disorder to be diagnosed. Insurance companies and HMOs may only budget a few minutes for the doctor to see his or her patients. It is often difficult for primary care physicians like general practitioners, family doctors, gynecologists, or internists to make a bipolar diagnosis if they have not seen many patients with bipolar disorder or if it has been many years since they saw bipolar patients in medical school. Therapists usually have not been trained in formal medical or psychiatric diagnoses.

Why did I have to go through all my life being sick when medications make me normal?

This is the first question many bipolar patients ask themselves after they begin to receive effective treatment and their bipolar symptoms subside. The next reaction is usually anger and indignation that so many people are unnecessarily forced to experience the iniquities of this illness, usually for years, because it was not diagnosed or treated.

BIPOLAR DISORDER IN OUR CULTURE

Much of the stigma of bipolar disorder is based on fear of the different. Unfortunately, people with bipolar disorder contribute to this stigma by unjustified embarrassment over their illness.

Why do people feel uncomfortable about bipolar disorder?

The very existence of bipolar disorder is a reminder to everyone else that they have their own mental and emotional problems. Chronic illnesses and injuries are not so threatening when patients have visible signs of illness such as consumption, bandages, or scars. It is easy to distance oneself from these poor wretches, but bipolar individuals are often attractive, intelligent, and successful. It can be terrifying to others to admit that they, too, could be vulnerable to illness.

What are some popular misconceptions about bipolar disorder?

Television and films usually depict persons with bipolar disorder as violent beasts with strange ideas and immoral behavior. Alternatively, bipolar individuals are sometimes characterized as mystics with special psychic powers or as special messengers from God or the devil.

How can we get rid of stigma?

Stigma is fueled by ignorance and fear. When the population is more aware of the true nature of bipolar disease, stigma will ebb.

Does our culture value bipolar attributes?

Definitely. While many people malign those with bipolar disorder, our culture almost worships manic symptoms like boundless energy, magnetic charisma, workaholia, the ability to go without sleep, hyperverbosity, and insatiable sexual appetite. If you think about it, you will see that these attributes fit most of the heroes and heroines that appear on our film and video screens. In real life, however, this pattern of attributes is caused by bipolar illness, and it damages people's lives rather than enhancing them.

I read in a book that bipolar disorder makes you smarter and more creative. Haven't famous people been bipolar?

I think that gestalt, a viewpoint that strives to see everything at the same time, and parallel thinking, the ability to processes similar thoughts at the same time, are often well developed in people with bipolar disorder. These talents can enhance problem solving and increase creativity, but the illness conspires to keep the bipolar individual from using their talents. There have long been unproven speculations that geniuses like Dostoyevsky, van Gogh, Orson Welles, and many others suffered from bipolar disorder. Although they became prominent historical figures, their lives were often filled with tragedy.

An Internet site said that world leaders like Julius Caesar, Henry VIII, and Mussolini were bipolars. How could you tell?

Try looking throughout history for charismatic, magnetic leaders with boundless energy, little need for sleep, wordiness, and an unquenchable sexual desire, who deteriorated as they aged. Were they bipolar? You can make up your own mind.

What is the cost of bipolar disorder to our society?

Bipolar disorder is among the top ten causes of disability all over the world. Millions of public dollars are spent for hospitalization and medical care that would never have been necessary if people's bipolar illness had been recognized and treated early. Homes are split, loves lost, fortunes squandered, and children made to suffer. There is no end to the toll that untreated bipolar disorder takes on all peoples of the world.

Do you think that the economy exploits people with bipolar disorder?

Absolutely. Knowingly or unknowingly, many businesses prey on bipolar individuals. For example, home shopping channels thrive on the bipolar tendency toward impulsive spending sprees. Liquor manufacturers' advertisements stressing power, wealth, fame, and sex appeal particularly to bipolars, who are at increased risk for developing alcohol problems. Casinos' mixture of grandiosity, free alcohol, and late hours prey on the manic tendency toward gambling and sexual addiction. Corrupt online casinos take advantage of bipolar obsessiveness and willingness to trust others. Pornographic Internet sites take advantage of bipolar impulsivity, hypersexuality, and the need for high stimulus levels and immediate gratification. "Too-good-to-be-true" offers of free loans, weight-loss schemes, and exotic cures prey on bipolar fantasies of perfection and hopes for a quick fix. Exploitation of bipolar illness is a gravy train for morally and ethically barren businesses and schemers.

What can I do to help other people with bipolar disorder?

When their bipolar disorder is under control, many people with bipolar illness feel that they have some responsibility to help others. Join national associations that advocate for bipolar individuals in the Congress and in state legislatures. Read bipolar newsletters and magazines published by national organizations and become familiar with the medical and social issues affecting bipolar individuals. Write letters to legislators, doctors' and therapists' organizations, and pharmaceutical companies. Go to bipolar meetings and speak out in support groups. Go to Internet chat and support sites, and tell others what you have learned that works for you. Your brothers and sisters with bipolar disorder need you.

2.

HEALTHY LIFE CHANGES
YOU SHOULD MAKE
NOW TO DECREASE
BIPOLAR SYMPTOMS

. . . .

I estimate that, once optimal bipolar medications and therapy are implemented, changing lifestyle and health patterns is the best thing you can do to improve your health. I believe that lifestyle changes can reduce residual bipolar symptoms by 10 to 30 percent. Best of all, lifestyle changes are easy to make, safe, and completely free of cost.

Overall, I have found that drinking alcohol, staying up all night, missing meals, and working too much are the most common behaviors that destabilize bipolar disorder.

STRESS DRIVES BIPOLAR DISORDER

Bipolar disorder is a stress-related disease. That is, the symptoms of bipolar disorder become worse as stress increases. Therefore, the most important thing that you can do is to purge the sources of stress from your life and make a commitment to keep new stressors under control. Effective stress treatment can be a godsend for bipolar sufferers: It is an effective means of helping to control bipolar illness that is both safe and free.

Unfortunately, stress reduction is often the most difficult treatment to convince patients to follow. When I tell patients to lower their stress levels they usually come up with excuses explaining why it is impossible. They say, "I couldn't possibly cut my workday by two hours," or, "I have to stay up until 3:00 A.M. every night," or, "I have to take on this extra work. I don't have a choice." The most common thing I hear is, "Don't worry, doctor, I'll be free from stress as soon as I finish this big project." Unfortunately, as each stressful project is finished, another one seems to take its place. It is important to remember that you can always find reasons why reducing stress seems difficult or impossible. Nevertheless, you must make your health a priority in your life in order to beat bipolar disorder.

What is stress anyway?

Stress refers to a physiological reaction of the body that overstimulates the adrenal glands, resulting in the overproduction of body stress steroid hormones such as cortisol and stress neurochemicals such as adrenaline. Among other things, these body stress biochemicals increase blood pressure and change blood flow, heart reactivity, urinary and bowel function, breathing rate, body temperature, perspiration, tremor, memory, and attention. Stress hormones are meant to be released only briefly in times of stress. However, modern life stresses are often constant. When stress steroids are present continuously in high concentrations, they produce permanent, unhealthy changes in the body and brain. Some studies have even shown that steroid hormones can kill brain cells when present at high levels for a prolonged period of time.

What are some examples of stress that can affect the body?

Examples of stress include working too many hours, not getting enough sleep, going to sleep too late, working under pressure or at the last moment, having or nearly having an accident, and so forth. Stress may also come from intense, pleasant experiences such as getting married, having a birthday, taking a trip, or having a child.

How much stress do I have to cut out of my life to be healthy again?

I recommend you start by spending 25 percent less time in activities that cause you stress. For example, if work is the main source of your stress and you work seven days a week, cut back to five. If you are working fifty-five hours per week, cut back to forty. Believe me, you can do it.

What is the connection between stress, bipolar disorder, and the immune system?

The exact connection is not clear, although the immune, hormonal, and neurotransmitter systems are very closely interconnected. For example, an injection of naturally occurring immune system compounds (called inflammatory cytokines) can trigger depression. So can the administration of stress hormones involved in the immune response.

How can I be under stress? I like working all night long with no sleep.

Stress refers to things that overstimulate our bodies. The secretion of stress steroids makes our hearts beat faster, our blood pressure rise, our hands shake, our body sweat, and our stomach acid churn. It really does not matter whether you like something or not; it can still cause damage to your body and health.

Try going to a bipolar support group or online forum and notice how much outside stressors increase other people's bipolar symptoms and severity.

If I reduce the stress in my life, will I be able to cut back on my medication?

You probably would not have to take much medication if you moved to Siberia and lived alone in a Quonset hut, eating bonbons and watching

MTV all day. However, most people with bipolar disorder choose to live a more complex life with higher levels of stress. If you choose to live a life with typical amounts of stress, you will probably have to take medications *and* manage your life stresses to keep yourself healthy.

STRESS REDUCTION AND RELAXATION TECHNIQUES

I suggest that you learn one or more relaxation techniques, such as muscle relaxation or meditation. You can do relaxation exercises daily to reduce your overall stress level. When you know you will have something stressful to deal with, you can practice your relaxation exercise beforehand. If all else fails and you find yourself in the middle of a stressful situation, you can excuse yourself for a moment, and do your relaxation exercise. There is no better way to learn to cope with stress.

What are muscle relaxation techniques?

Muscle relaxation training refers to a variety of physical exercises for relaxing your body and mind. Here is one I use. Sit comfortably in a chair. Now tense all the muscles in your toes, feet, and legs. Tighten the muscles as hard as you can while breathing in slowly, then breathe out slowly and relax them. Next, tighten the muscles in your hips and abdomen as hard as you can while inhaling slowly. Hold your breath for a moment, then exhale slowly and relax those muscles. Now, tighten all the muscles in your fingers and arms while you breathe in slowly. Hold your breath momentarily, then exhale and relax. Finally, tighten the muscles in your shoulders, neck, and face and breathe in slowly. Once again, hold your breath for a moment, then relax and exhale. Now notice your breathing. As you slowly breathe in, imagine you are gathering together all the stress in your body. Then breathe out slowly and exhale all your stress along with your breath. You should continue this breathing for at least a minute, although you can do it longer if you like. You can use this technique regularly, twice a day, or any time you have to deal with a stressful event.

What is meditation and how can I use it to manage stress?

Meditation refers to a diverse collection of mental, emotional, and physical exercises that have been devised over the last several thousand years for the purpose of changing the way we experience our lives by increasing our control over our thoughts, feelings, and physical bodies. Meditation can be useful in bipolar disorder to aid relaxation and reduce stress as well as to exercise our ability to focus and control our stream of consciousness.

Are there simple meditations that you recommend to your patients?

I have a special design printed on my business cards so my patients can use them as the simplest possible meditation tool. Feel free to copy this page and cut out the card below so you can take it with you everywhere.

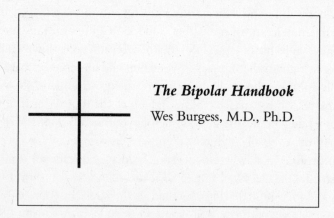

The Bipolar Handbook
Wes Burgess, M.D., Ph.D.

Begin by looking at the crossed lines on our card. Use your imagination to visualize that the two crossed lines form a tiny, perfect square where they intersect. Look hard until you see this tiny square and then focus your concentration on this point. Any time you notice some stray thoughts or emotions that distract you, transfer them to the little square until that is the only thing in your consciousness. Try this for thirty seconds several times a day, and bring the card with you to potentially stressful environments so that you can relax yourself before you become stressed.

Another simple form of meditation is based on breathing. Sit quietly and breathe in slowly, counting to five. Then exhale slowly at the same rate. Try doing this for sixty seconds at least twice a day and whenever you know you will be facing extra stress. You can slowly increase the time that you do this exercise, but do not push yourself. This is not a contest; it is about achieving relaxation, health, and inner peace.

Meditation is often associated with Eastern religions, but I have found that it can be compatible with all sorts of faiths when it is used as a relaxation exercise for our minds, emotions, and bodies. If you are unsure of how the practice of meditation fits with your religious beliefs, try to find a church representative who is knowledgeable about meditation and ask her or him.

Is there a meditation that can help me overcome obsessive thoughts?

Zazen is a form of meditation where all of your thoughts leave your mind and your consciousness is clear. If you can master it, then it can help you halt obsessions and expunge unwanted thoughts anytime throughout your day. Some people can do it naturally. Try sitting in a quiet place and clear your mind of thoughts. When a thought comes, look at it and then dismiss it and look for the next thought. At some point, the thoughts will stop coming and your mind will be clear.

You may want to seek outside help in learning this kind of meditation. Although zazen is often associated with Zen Buddhism, it is an exercise and not a religion. I have known of priests, ministers, pastors, and agnostics who have all learned and value the zazen technique. There are some informative books on Zen in chapter 10 to get you started.

Remember, performing these relaxation meditations is like practicing any other exercise. The more often you do them, the easier they will be and the more you will benefit from them. Go slow at the beginning, stop before you get tired, and build up your meditation times gradually.

What if I can't stop my wandering thoughts?
  My mind is racing.

If you can't keep intrusive thoughts out of your mind no matter what you do, then you are too distractible and your thoughts are too repetitive and obsessive. The next step is to talk to your doctor and make sure you are taking enough mood stabilizer(s) or other bipolar medications that can stop intrusive thoughts.

What about hypnosis? I think that would
  work for me if it were safe.

I do not recommend hypnosis for bipolar disorder. In bipolar illness, we are always working to improve control of thoughts and emotions, whereas hypnosis is a process of relinquishing control.

SLEEPERS, AWAKE!
SLEEP AND BIPOLAR DISORDER

Sleep disturbance is an intrinsic component of bipolar disorder. It can take the form of periodic or lifetime problems getting to sleep, staying asleep, or waking up. During inactivated periods of the illness, sleep problems are usually manifested as difficulty getting up in the morning and a desire to sleep during the day, called hypersomnia. In bipolar depression, where hypersomnia combines with symptoms of fatigue and low motivation, many patients end up feeling that the only thing wrong is that they need a good night's sleep. Ultimately, the solution is to treat the underlying bipolar disorder that is causing the sleep problems and then the symptoms will get better.

In mania, the inability to get to sleep is often exacerbated by purposefully staying up all night, watching television, surfing the Internet, or engaging in other stimulating activities. I remember interviewing a young bipolar woman who had come to me for insomnia. I asked her, "What is it exactly that keeps you from falling asleep?" "It is usually the headphones or a video game," she said dryly. "I make myself stay up all night."

Can insomnia trigger a bipolar episode?

One of the surest ways to trigger manic symptoms is to stay up for twenty-four hours or more. Conversely, my experience has shown that adequate, regular sleep reduces the symptoms of bipolar disorder.

My problem is that I sleep too long in the morning. I need a pill to wake me up.

When I hear this, I usually find that the problem comes from going to bed too late. If you go to bed in the early morning hours, there is nothing that can help you get up in the morning because you simply aren't getting enough sleep. Go to sleep early and after a few days, you will find it easier to get up on time. If you cannot stay asleep then lie in bed quietly with your eyes closed.

However, if you find you are sleeping ten or more hours a day, you may be suffering from bipolar depression. Sometimes, you may have to wait for the depression to ebb before excess sleepiness goes away. Discuss this with your doctor and see if your bipolar disorder can be treated more effectively to minimize this problem.

My uncle told me that if I stay up twenty-four hours straight, my sleep problems would be cured.

This technique may be helpful for some people who do not suffer from bipolar illness, but staying up all night is one sure way to worsen bipolar disorder and detract from your health in general. Nevertheless, it is very attractive advice to manics who want to stay up anyway. After almost twenty years of helping patients through their sleep problems, believe me; it only makes matters worse.

Q I don't have to sleep anymore, and I still have
     energy! I'm ecstatic! It feels like a gift
     from God.

Mania prompts many individuals with bipolar disorder to feel that they do
not need any sleep or only a few hours of sleep a night. Nevertheless, nobody can stay healthy if they do not get an adequate night's sleep. Insufficient rest produces an excess strain on the body, interferes with performance,
impairs memory, lowers the seizure threshold, and probably shortens your
life span. The solution is to strengthen your bipolar treatment so that the
mania subsides, and your sleep will become more normal.

Q Six months ago, I couldn't wake up. Now
     I can't get to sleep. What's the deal?

This may be a sign that you are starting a manic cycle. First, check whether
there are any manic triggers such as stress, drugs, or alcohol use that you can
reduce by yourself. Then ask your doctor if you should have stronger bipolar medications to block a manic episode.

HOW TO GET A GOOD NIGHT'S SLEEP

Part of the genesis of bipolar symptoms appears to be a disturbance in
the internal biological clocks that keep our body systems in synchroniza-
tion. Many persons with bipolar disorder describe symptoms that resemble
jet lag, which we know is a desynchronization of biological clocks. By
keeping an appropriate sleep/wake schedule and sticking to it religiously,
you help keep your body systems running in unison.

I suggest that you go to bed at the same time every night—preferably
between ten and eleven o'clock. Similarly, I advise you to pick a time to rise
in the morning and stick to it every day. Open the curtains and turn on lots
of lights when you wake up so that your body gets plenty of clues that it is
morning. It is surprising how many people find they feel better or cycle less

frequently when they adhere to this schedule. Note: If you change the schedule on the weekend, it may not work as well for you during the week.

I'm used to going out in the evenings and having some fun. When will I see my friends?

You cannot keep a healthy sleep schedule and still stay out late every night with your friends. It may seem that your friends can stay healthy on three hours of sleep per night, but you cannot and neither can most of the population. Before you think of reasons why a strict sleep schedule will be difficult, try out the schedule approach and see how much better you feel.

What is valerian, and is it okay for me to take it with bipolar disorder?

Valerian is an herbal root extract of the plant named *Valeriana officinalis* that has been used for generations as a sleeping aid. None of my bipolar patients has reported problems with it, but it may not be strong enough to reverse your insomnia.

I read the term "sleep hygiene" on the Internet. What is it?

Professionals at sleep clinics often recommend a protocol for ensuring that your sleep space is comfortable and conducive to uninterrupted sleep. They call this "sleep hygiene." For example, good sleep hygiene would entail making sure that your bed is comfortable, your bedroom is quiet, and the temperature is clement. Sleep clinics usually recommend that you sleep only in your bedroom, and that you not use your bedroom for reading or watching television, so that every time you go there your body is signaled that it is time to sleep.

It is of the utmost importance to make sure you are not interrupted during your sleep. Let voicemail or an answering machine take your telephone calls at night and do not get up to check your e-mail. If you do need to get up in the middle of the night, go back to bed immediately. I have often heard people say, "I didn't think I would get back to sleep so I just stayed up all night and watched television." This only builds bad habits.

Is there anything I should have in my bedroom to help me sleep?

I find that a source of noise helps many people sleep, including me. Inexpensive fans work well, and special noise-generating units are available at a variety of prices. Some people like big, soft pillows to hang onto; others prefer thin pillows and a hard bed. The key is finding what is most comfortable to you.

Are there any over-the-counter medications that can help solve my sleep problem?

Diphenhydramine (Benadryl) is an antihistamine that is often used to induce sleep, and I have found that when it is used on an occasional basis it won't destabilize bipolar disorder. However, it leaves some people drowsy the next day. Benadryl that includes a decongestant could cause jittery feelings, so be sure to stick to products that only contain diphenhydramine.

Would eating or exercising help my sleep?

You should not eat close to bedtime if you have bipolar disorder, to prevent untoward weight gain. Moderate exercise, like walking around the block, helps some people sleep but not all. Check it out for yourself.

I heard that steam baths are good for bipolar disorder. What do you think?

Many people who suffer from bipolar disorder have told me that they feel better in a very hot bathtub, sauna, or steam room. I cannot personally account for this, but I know that hot baths help some people sleep.

What method do you suggest for falling asleep?

I suggest that you go to bed, turn off the lights, close your eyes, and let your mind be clear of thoughts for thirty minutes. Use the meditation and relaxation exercises we discussed earlier in this chapter. If your head is still too full of thoughts, I suggest that you meet with your doctor and see if you need to strengthen your bipolar medicines.

If you're such an expert, what do *you* do to get to sleep?

I get in bed, close my eyes, and imagine that I have just inherited an apartment house and I have to meet all the tenants. Going from door to door introducing myself is so boring that I fall right to sleep. Try using this fantasy to block out the worried and annoying thoughts that are keeping you awake.

SLEEPING PILLS AND ALCOHOL

Unfortunately, our culture has incorporated the notion of sleeping pills into everybody's daily lives. Many people automatically think of taking a pill if they do not get right to sleep or wake up during the night. All sleeping pills, both prescription and over-the-counter, contain sedatives that can actually disturb the natural sleep cycle of dreaming and deep sleep that is necessary for rest.

Will over-the-counter nighttime and sleeping products that I buy in the drugstore help me sleep?

I think that the sleeping pills that are available in the drugstore are worthless at best. Depending on their formulation, they may even worsen your bipolar illness. Stay away from them.

Will prescription sleeping pills help regulate my sleep cycle?

In bipolar disorder, the effects of prescription sleeping pills often diminish in a few weeks' time. Doses may have to be raised again and again, bringing about drug dependence and worsening insomnia. I have seen many people with bipolar disorder that were addicted to sleeping pills such as zolpidem (Ambien). In my opinion, sedatives do not solve problems in bipolar disorder and they may cause new problems of their own.

Will a glass of wine before bed help me feel drowsy?

Alcohol is the most common substance people take to help them sleep, but it is also the major cause of insomnia in this country. Most people can drink themselves to sleep if they try hard enough. However, alcohol upsets the dreaming sleep cycle and actually causes insomnia on subsequent days. A colleague once showed me brain wave recordings of sleeping individuals (called sleep EEGs) where evidence of alcohol's effects on sleep was visible weeks after the last drink was taken. You should also be aware that mixing sleeping pills with alcohol could be a deadly mistake.

NUTRITION AND WEIGHT LOSS

People with bipolar disorder tend to gain and lose weight precipitously. Individuals often gain weight when they are depressed and lose weight when they are manic. Both depression and weight gain tend to increase with age if nothing is done to stop them. During manic episodes, some are pleased with their lack of appetite and ability to lose weight, but trying to become manic as a method of weight control can be deadly.

Sometimes people with bipolar disorder develop eating habits that interfere with losing weight. The most common habits I have seen in bipolar disorder are eating late at night and eating breakfast food cereals. I have known several people who were so adamant about having their midnight bowl of cereal that they could never lose weight.

How does eating affect my bipolar disorder?

It is not completely understood how food and diet affect bipolar disorder. It is apparent that missing meals and starving yourself causes bodily stress, which is probably not good for bipolar disorder. Bipolar disorder also sends your body distorted signals that may cause you to crave certain foods. Furthermore, certain foods can affect the way you feel. For example, I have heard from many people with bipolar disorder that their mood can change radically for the better after eating chocolate, carbohydrates, or even a very large meal.

There is no special diet or nutritional scheme that can effectively treat bipolar disorder. However, my impression is that a diet high in protein and low in starch will not worsen bipolar disorder and may help it. I recommend high-quality proteins like beef and lamb and low-fat protein sources such as turkey, chicken, fish, nonfat cottage cheese, yogurt, and low-fat cheeses like ricotta, farmer's cheese, and Mexican cheese. Eggs are high in protein and easy to fix.

The most important recommendation is that you eat a healthy, nutritionally balanced diet. If you are having problems adhering to healthy eating habits, ask your doctor to recommend a qualified nutritionist.

Why do I crave chocolate? Does it have anything to do with bipolar disorder?

Chocolate contains compounds like theobromine, caffeine, and trigonelline, which artificially stimulate the body by increasing adrenaline. Another component, called phenylethylamine, is structurally similar to addictive drugs such as amphetamines.

Does sugar worsen bipolar symptoms?

Many patients have told me that they feel hyperactive or manicky after eating "sugar," but I have never found anyone who could get a "sugar high" from eating spoonfuls of table sugar. Therefore, I suspect something else is involved when people feel hyperactive after eating. In addition to sugar, most candies contain a stimulant in the form of chocolate. Health and power bars are similar, with a lot of starch added in the form of grains. Doughnuts, cake, and pie are heavy on starch and fat in addition to sugar. If these make you feel hyper, then stay away from them.

Why do I feel so hopeless about my weight loss?

It is common in bipolar disorder to be extra concerned about your outward appearance. Many with the disorder feel that they cannot go out of the house until they lose weight or that no one will want to associate with a fat person. The burden to lose weight then inhibits those with bipolar disorder from socializing, meeting people, making friends, or applying for a better job.

You will enjoy your life better if you start going out now, before you lose all your weight.

Will going on a diet affect my bipolar disorder? What do you think about the Atkins diet and the South Beach diet?

My bipolar patients are using high-protein diets and losing weight. So far, I have not seen these diets destabilize bipolar disorder. If you have bipolar disorder, you should always discuss your personal health concerns with a doctor before you start a diet, to make sure the plan you choose is right for you.

What else can I do about my weight?

Look into national associations for bipolar disorder, professional and personal websites, and online forums. Talk about your weight issues with other persons with bipolar disorder and find out what works and what does not.

What about diet pills? I heard that if I take them, I can eat all I want and still lose weight.

Sorry. There are no magic weight-loss schemes. The notion of eating everything you want and losing weight is nothing more than a fantasy made up to sell phony diet pills. So is the advertisement that claims that you will lose weight without exercise. In fact, stimulant diet pills such as phentermine (Adipex and Ionamin), benzphetamine (Didrex), and methamphetamine (Desoxyn), as well as herbal stimulants, can worsen depression and trigger mania or psychosis in persons with bipolar disorder. Many people like the energy that diet pills give them, but stimulants in the pills can also cause insomnia and put a strain on the heart. It is important that you stay away from them. To get more energy and lose weight, the healthiest and most effective options are to watch your diet and exercise regularly.

My doctor said my weight is endangering my health. Is there a safe medication I can take that can help me regain my health?

There is a prescription medication called orlistat (Xenical) that reduces the amount of fat the body absorbs from food and can be given to those who are severely overweight. My patients who have taken this medication have had success losing weight but progress is slow. Patients in research studies were still losing weight six months after beginning the medication and had not gained it back. This is an important hurdle because it is generally believed that if you can keep weight off for six months, it is much less likely to come back. Patients taking orlistat have also been able to start programs of exercise and diet that had been impossible for them before.

Some people taking orlistat will get gas, cramping, and/or diarrhea and will be unable to take the medicine. Consult a doctor who is familiar with orlistat and its use.

VITAMINS, HERBS, AND SUPPLEMENTS

After years of continued reading and research, I can say conclusively that bipolar disorder and its symptoms cannot be cured with vitamins or supplements. This does not stop manufacturers and salespeople from making claims, however. It is your job to find out enough about bipolar disorder and health supplements that you can take advantage of any health benefits they might provide without being scammed. Always beware of magazines, websites, and practitioners who derive income from the sale of the products that they recommend.

What is the simplest vitamin program that you recommend?

I recommend a simple and inexpensive supplement plan to promote general health. "Once daily" type vitamins are available by brand name or as generic store brands in most drugstores and supermarkets. I recommend taking two of these "once daily" vitamins every morning for your general nutrition. This should help ensure that your body is getting plenty of vitamins without going overboard.

Are there effective herbal treatments for bipolar disorder? Are they safe?

There have been claims that evening primrose oil (EPO) may be of some help in decreasing the fatigue of bipolar depression, but none of my patients ever felt it was helpful enough to continue taking it. Many of my patients are taking omega fatty acids and fish oil supplements. These may be helpful for general cardiac health but they have never been shown to benefit bipolar disorder.

Most herbs do have side effects and potential interactions with other medications and other supplements. It depends on the situation and the dose. Check with your doctor first to see if a specific herbal product will worsen your condition or interact with the medications you take.

Are the herbs and supplements sold on the Internet safe for me to buy?

Much of the information about herbal remedies on the Internet and from other sources can be confusing and misleading. The best reference I have found is the Natural Medicines Comprehensive Database at http://www.naturaldatabase.com. Their service is somewhat expensive but maybe you could get your doctor to sign up and let you use the service. Buying herbs or supplements on the Internet can also be dangerous, as you never know exactly what is in the supplements you are buying. Talk to your doctor about which brands are reliable.

Several health professionals have offered to sell me glandular extracts for mood and energy. Do they work?

Dried preparations of cow and pig glands have been promoted for years but usually have little potency. Besides, the whole thing sounds disgusting to me.

Is there any problem if I take large amounts of vitamin A (beta-carotene)?

Taking too much vitamin A can be harmful, particularly to your liver. Major studies suggest that beta-carotene can increase the risk of getting lung cancer. And there is at least one account in the literature of a person who died from eating prodigious amounts of vitamin A. So, do not go overboard. Talk with your doctor about finding the dosage for your needs.

Q I have heard that Saint-John's-wort is an effective treatment for depression. Is it effective for those with bipolar depression?

Saint-John's-wort (*Hypericum perforatum*) has been widely used in Europe and even in the United States as a natural treatment for unipolar major depression. However, the jury is still out on its effectiveness. A large, well-controlled United States study found no benefit for depression. Some of my bipolar patients have reported feeling edgy and anxious when taking the herb.

If you decide to try Saint-John's-wort, consult with your family doctor or psychiatrist first. Saint-John's-wort has numerous counter-indications and drug interactions, and it may make the skin more vulnerable to sun and thus to skin cancer.

Q My brother takes ginseng for energy. Is this stuff any good for bipolar disorder?

Panax ginseng is promoted as a stimulant with many health benefits. However, its stimulant actions may be bad for bipolar disorder. I know of one report where a man took moderate doses of *Panax ginseng* that triggered a psychotic, manic episode so severe that he had to go to the hospital.

Q My sports doctor recommended high colonics to take out the poisons that cause bipolar disorder. Are there any dangers to this?

I know of no poisons that cause bipolar disorder. Historically, enemas have been promoted for a wealth of physical and mental problems, but there is no evidence for their effectiveness with bipolar disorder.

EXERCISE

Regular, appropriate exercise is important for heart and lung health, weight control, and combating fatigue. Patients tell me that a regular and reasonable (not excessive) amount of exercise helps with depression and anxiety.

Should I have an exercise plan?

I suggest exercising three times a week for twenty to forty-five minutes each day. If this is too much for you, then start gradually.

Can too much exercise make bipolar disorder worse?

Too much exercise—for example, aggressive workouts lasting five hours daily, seven days a week—can help trigger a bipolar episode and/or maintain a state of mania. Excessive exercise can also cause changes in hormonal secretion, cartilage loss, musculoskeletal changes, and orthopedic problems. It is sometimes hard to tell if people are driving themselves into mania by overexercising or if they start exercising excessively when they begin to get manic. I recommend sticking to a moderate exercise program in order to guard against triggering an episode, and to beware of times when you feel the need to work out excessively, as it could be an indication that you are entering a manic phase.

Can I stop taking my medications if my exercise is making me feel better?

Exercise helps many people feel invigorated and more emotionally balanced, but exercise alone is not enough to control bipolar disorder. It is important that you continue to take your medications in addition to adopting a healthy exercise program.

What do you think about sports drinks or power drinks for bipolar disorder?

Most of the ones I have examined look like sugar water. For the most part, I think drinking plain, clean water is the best choice. If you are in danger of being dehydrated, drink fluid and try taking salt pills or drink salted tomato juice. This will help increase the volume of fluid in your body.

Doesn't exercise cure depression? I've read that it does in several national magazines.

Exercise is good for you, but it will not "cure" bipolar depression.

CAFFEINE, ALCOHOL, DRUGS, AND TOBACCO

Our culture encourages many unhealthy and potentially addicting habits, including the use of caffeine, alcohol, cigarettes, and drugs such as marijuana. Unfortunately, these substances may be especially unhealthy for persons with bipolar disorder because they can increase bipolar symptoms and even trigger bipolar episodes. It is very encouraging to see bipolar sufferers' treatment success improve after they are able to give up these unhealthy habits. Fortunately, many people with bipolar disorder lose interest in their unhealthy habits when their mood stabilizers are well adjusted.

I drink lots of coffee. Is coffee bad for you if you have bipolar disorder?

Many of my patients have noticed a distinct improvement in their stability when they stopped drinking coffee. High-dose caffeine has been reported to trigger manic and psychotic symptoms. Some people with bipolar disorder enjoy the "jazzed up" feeling that caffeine gives them, but this is not necessarily a good thing. The goal for anyone struggling with bipolar disorder should be peace, contentment, and fulfillment, and these do not require caffeine.

Caffeine is addicting, and it provokes a withdrawal syndrome when stopped. Coffee is the most serious offender involved in caffeine addiction. Iced teas can contain enough stimulant alkaloids to affect your health if you drink enough, and the caffeine content in colas can also create a problem. The tablets that are sold over-the-counter to help you stay awake contain large amounts of caffeine.

If you are addicted to caffeine and stop taking it suddenly, you may experience withdrawal. Withdrawal symptoms like fatigue and a flu-like sensation may last for two days or more. However, many patients feel so much more stable after they've stopped drinking coffee that they never return to drinking it. A few days of possible discomfort are a small price to pay for a lifetime of improved health.

Is drinking alcohol bad for bipolar disorder?

Individuals with bipolar disorder often react to alcohol as if it were a stimulant, making them more mentally active, happy, charming, and sociable when they drink. Ultimately, it resembles the stimulating effects of mania. This positive experience makes drinking alcohol more pleasant, but it can also cause substance abuse problems for those with the disorder. Eighty percent of all people with bipolar disorder will suffer from an alcohol and/or drug problem during their lifetime. Alcohol in large doses is toxic to the brain and body, and ingestion of sufficient alcohol can trigger mania, depression, or even psychosis.

Nearly all medications used for bipolar disorder carry a warning against drinking alcohol. But skipping your medications when you know you will be consuming alcohol is not a good option, either. In my opinion, those with bipolar disorder should not consume more than one drink per month. Many people find that it is easier to control their drinking by stopping altogether. It is often difficult for those with bipolar disorder to give up alcohol, but consumption can be an impediment to successful bipolar treatment. I have worked with several people whose unwillingness to stop one or two daily drinks made their disease virtually untreatable. Fortunately, many people lose the desire to drink once their medication doses are well balanced.

I'm worried that if I stop drinking, I'll lose all my friends. What can I do?

It is possible to drink nonalcoholic beverages when you go out, and your friends may support your decision. However, people who try to stop drinking often find that their drinking buddies care more about getting drunk themselves than they care about other people and their health. If you socialize with people who will abandon you if you stop drinking, then you need to get better friends.

I go to Alcoholics Anonymous. Does this program work in bipolar disorder?

Yes. Many of my bipolar patients have reversed their drinking problems by participating in AA. There are usually meetings in most hospitals and elsewhere in the community. Odds are that you will not be the only person with bipolar disorder there.

I smoke marijuana every day, and it's better than any medication. Can this help my bipolar disorder?

I have heard this many times before. Marijuana apparently makes bipolar symptoms more tolerable, but it destabilizes the illness in the long run. Marijuana may contribute to depression, lung disease, and loss of memory, as well as deplete sex hormones. Moreover, using it is illegal. These reasons are enough to convince me that marijuana is not worth the risk if you have bipolar disorder.

Even in small doses, marijuana can undermine bipolar treatment. Many people with bipolar disorder are affected by one or two puffs of a joint.

What problems do cigarettes cause among people with bipolar illness?

There are instances in the literature where too much tobacco smoking has triggered bouts of mania and psychosis in persons with bipolar disorder. In addition, smoking can significantly decrease the amount of medication that reaches the bloodstream, interfering with effective treatment. Cigarettes are the proven offenders in these cases, but I suspect that the risks are similar whether you smoke cigars or pipes or chew tobacco. No one can say for sure how much tobacco someone with bipolar disorder can tolerate safely. However, we do know that tobacco shortens life and causes heart disease, lung disease, and cancer. Why should you take any chances with your health? If you do smoke, check with your doctor to see how your medications are affected by smoking and try to give up the habit.

I have tried to quit before, and it is so difficult. How can I quit for good?

If you cannot stop, then you may be rushing yourself. Many people sabotage themselves by trying to do everything at once, before they lose their nerve. However, learning not to smoke is a gradual process. You need to develop daily skills to ensure you can go without smoking for the rest of your life. Fortunately, many of my patients have stopped smoking on their own after their medications were in order. To those who are ready to get serious about kicking the habit, I have developed an effective method for giving up cigarettes (see next page).

HEALTH FADS

Popular ideas about what is healthy change with the times, and many popularized health notions can be harmful. For example, a bipolar man came to see me one day at the insistence of his wife. He said he knew he was healthy because he followed all the popular advice. Every day he worked

HOW TO STOP SMOKING PAINLESSLY

. . . . . .

If you have tried to stop smoking cold turkey and failed, or if you just do not want to endure the bodily stress and physical discomfort usually associated with smoking cessation, follow the steps below. Most likely, you will be able to reduce or stop your smoking habit without gaining weight or suffering severe cigarette craving.

- Set a goal of quitting entirely or decide how many cigarettes you want to end up smoking.
- Find an empty pack or buy a cigarette box to hold all the cigarettes you will smoke each day.
- Count how many cigarettes you currently smoke per day and subtract one from that number.
- For the first week, put that number of cigarettes in your pack every day.
- Just smoke the cigarettes you put in your pack each day, no more and no less.
- The next week, subtract one from the daily number of cigarettes you smoked last week and put that number of cigarettes in your pack each day.
- Again, just smoke the cigarettes you put in your pack each day, no more and no less, for a week.
- Continue smoking one less cigarette each week until you reach your goal.

For example, if you are now smoking twenty cigarettes daily, reduce to nineteen the first week, eighteen the second week, seventeen the third week, and so on. You will have broken your habit and be smoke-free in five months and your body will thank you.

out for five hours, he drank two quarts of water, he ate only health supplements, and he had lost fifty pounds. In reality, this tall man weighed about one hundred pounds, and he looked like a walking skeleton. His skin was pale and yellow, and he had deep circles under his eyes. When he was not working out, all he could do was pace around the house in anguish. He had tried to follow all the health advice in popular books and on television, but it had made him unhealthy instead.

I read about so many new alternative
treatments. Isn't there something fast
and easy?

It's hard to be patient if you have bipolar disorder, but there is no magic
health bullet or miracle treatment for bipolar illness. The best approach is to
practice moderation in your lifestyle and not waste your time and endanger
your health by chasing rainbows. Believe me, if there was something new,
effective, and safe for the treatment of bipolar disorder it would be all over
the medical press. Every doctor would want to get on the bandwagon to
treat bipolar disorder better.

Once I treated a group of friends who all had bipolar disorder. One day
I received a call, telling me that none of them would be coming back to my
office. They said that they were all taking green tea and they all felt better
than ever before. Green tea, they said, was better than any medication.
About six weeks later, they trickled back into my office to start their old
medications again. It turned out that they had all felt better drinking green
tea, but their bipolar disorder gradually worsened until they could not
function the way they should. Only then did they realize they needed to get
back on track.

Can I take nonprescription products that
I see in the drugstore, on television,
or on the Internet?

Over-the-counter (OTC) medications that are often labeled "safe" have
not been specifically tested on people with bipolar disorder. There are many
over-the-counter remedies that have been known to worsen bipolar symptoms, trigger mania, or even cause psychosis. These include decongestants,
asthma remedies, cough syrups, and cold medicines that contain adrenaline
(epinephrine) and similar compounds such as ephedrine, pseudoephedrine,
or phenylpropanolamine (which is now banned in the United States).

While many of my patients have described problems with antihistamine products, they are often necessary to relieve allergy symptoms. At this time, my patients seem to be doing best on plain loratadine (Claritin) without any added decongestant. Diphenhydramine (Benadryl) is my second choice for bipolar patients, but it can cause drowsiness.

SIX STEPS FOR REDUCING
BIPOLAR SYMPTOMS

1. Reduce your overall life stress.
2. Get enough quality sleep without oversleeping.
3. Adopt good eating habits and maintain a healthy weight as defined by your doctor.
4. Attend to your nutritional needs.
5. Exercise regularly in moderation.
6. Avoid habits and substances that worsen bipolar disorder, such as caffeine, alcohol, nicotine, and drugs.

3.

MEDICAL TREATMENT
FOR BIPOLAR DISORDER

. . . .

At this moment in medical history, successful bipolar treatment has to be grounded in medications. You will want to find out the medications that are available and understand their different advantages, so that you can discuss them with your doctor and help choose the ones that suit you best. We will discuss mood stabilizers, atypicals, antianxiety medications, and little-known medications that can help bipolar disorder. You will also find out about prescription medications that make bipolar disorder worse and should be avoided. You will discover soon-to-be-released bipolar medications that work in new and better ways, and you will see both new and proven medical treatments for bipolar disorder that do not involve taking medications at all.

MOOD STABILIZERS

Most of the medications that have been proved to help bipolar disorder belong to a class of medications called "mood stabilizers." Mood stabilizers reduce all bipolar symptoms by working directly on the brain cells that cause bipolar disorder, and they are the only bipolar treatment that is known to prevent manic or depressed episodes from occurring. Mood stabilizers stop the flow of unnecessary thoughts, help to remove mental "fog," and clear the mind. They can reduce distractibility and thus improve attention.

Mood stabilizers can control mood, minimize anxiety and agitation, and decrease the frequency and severity of angry episodes. Mood stabilizers allow your nervous system to function the way it was meant to so that you can become your most natural self.

Although there are many mood stabilizers available, there are only three that have been proven over the years to effectively treat bipolar disorder and prevent its recurrence: carbamazepine, valproate, and lithium salt.

What do mood stabilizers do in the brain?

All the medications in this class stabilize parts of the brain cell membranes (sodium channels) to keep brain cells firing at the normal rhythm. There is also some scientific evidence that carbamazepine, valproate, and lithium salt can help protect and/or grow new, healthy brain cells in adults. Some studies show that lamotrigine can also protect brain cells from damage. Mood stabilizers, especially carbamazepine, are often used after brain injury as part of the recovery process. The full implications of these findings are not yet appreciated.

Do mood stabilizers ever work miracles? I sure need one.

You may be in luck. Mood stabilizers can work quite quickly and dramatically in some people. In other cases, the effect may be delayed until the medication is at the right dose for you. In order to find the right dose, your doctor will start at a low dose and work up to higher amounts, giving your body a chance to acclimate to the medication.

What dosage will I have to take and how often will I need to take my medicine?

Carbamazepine and valproate are sometimes prescribed in small doses throughout the day, because this is the way they are used for treating seizures. However, for bipolar disorder, mood stabilizers can usually be given once daily, often before bedtime. Then, if there are any side effects, they occur during sleep.

How do you decide the optimal dose of bipolar medication?

I try to encourage a good working relationship with my patients where we both participate equally in making decisions. We discuss our progress and where we want the treatment to go and we make decisions accordingly. Often, patients can recognize the problems that bipolar disorder causes them and want to help raise their own medication dose to the optimum level. For patients who have not yet learned to recognize their disease symptoms, I make the lion's share of the decisions at first and try to draw them into the treatment as soon as possible.

Is deciding the dose just trial and error?

Absolutely not. I usually have a good idea of the range of expected doses that will be needed. However, the treatment is not for me, it is for you, the patient. For best results, you and your doctor have to work together.

My doctor wants to put me on several different medications. Is that reasonable?

It is generally a good idea to minimize the number of medicines that you take, but the majority of persons with bipolar disorder feel best taking a combination of two or more medications.

Of the top three mood stabilizers, which is least likely to cause weight gain?

In my experience, carbamazepine is less likely to cause weight gain than valproate or lithium salt. Reasonable eating habits and diet can compensate for medication effects, however. I work with many people taking mood stabilizers who keep themselves fashionably slim.

Why should I take medications that might have risks?

There is no free ticket to health. You have to compare the risks of any type of treatment with the risks of no treatment. There are dire consequences of not treating bipolar disorder, including losing one's job, friends, marriage, life savings, and self-respect. You know that there is some risk to driving on the highway, playing a sport, going on a trip, and so forth, but you still choose to do these activities. You have to compare the benefits of medications to the likelihood of risks whenever you make any decision.

Doctors are committed to telling you all the possible problems of the medication options they offer so that you can make a fair and informed decision about whether to take them or not.

Why should I put up with medication side effects when "natural" treatments are completely safe and have no side effects?

You should know that there are potentially severe or even fatal reactions to herbal products, health supplements, and high-dose vitamins even if nutritional advisors tell you otherwise. If you do not believe me, check the literature: there are cases of death from vitamin overdose, heart attacks precipitated from energy supplements, and so forth. Prescription medications, herbs, and supplements all have risks, but nonmedical practitioners are not required by law to tell you all the important risks stemming from the products they sell. Some may not even know all the potential risks.

Will a mood stabilizer keep me from being creative?

I work with many writers and performers in the entertainment industry who depend on their creativity to be successful. It sometimes takes them a bit of adjustment to get used to having control over their thoughts after starting mood stabilizers. However, when their medication is optimized, they have all told me that their creativity was as good as or (often) better than ever.

What medication can help me keep overwhelming thoughts out of my head?

Circular or intrusive thoughts are the bane of bipolar existence. They can distract you from your work and/or studies, keep you awake at night, and lead you into obsession. Mood stabilizers can relieve these intrusive thoughts, as can some atypical antipsychotics. Clonidine (Catapres) and trazodone (Desyrel) are other medications that sometimes help, but these are not licensed for use in bipolar disorder.

Which mood stabilizers are best for sleeping?

When insomnia is caused by bipolar disorder, any major mood stabilizer at the correct dose should help improve your sleep cycle.

How well do mood stabilizers work for depressed symptoms?

When bipolar disorder flares up, I give mood stabilizers to treat the underlying bipolar disorder that causes both depression and mania. Sometimes a depressive episode is hard to stop after it has already been triggered by a manic episode. However, mood stabilizers, alone or in combination, can help make depressed, inactivated symptoms much more tolerable until the depressive cycle is ended.

Carbamazepine, lithium salt, and lamotrigine have produced the best results against depression in my patients.

How do I know that a mood stabilizer will even work for me?

The overwhelming majority of bipolar individuals who can take an adequate dose of mood stabilizers are helped. Ultimately, you have to be the judge of what is helpful for you. In order to find out if you will be satisfied with a mood stabilizer, you will have to try it.

How will my doctor monitor my dosage?

Ultimately, there is no laboratory test level that can measure your health. The only way your doctor can tell if you are getting enough medication is to examine you and talk with you in his or her office.

In the case of carbamazepine, valproate, and lithium salt, your doctor will take occasional blood tests to determine the level of medication that is present in the bloodstream and the general health of the body. These are the only mood stabilizers for which blood tests are usually required.

Why do some drugs have two different names?

Every name brand medication has two names. The first is its generic name and the second is its brand name, which is capitalized. For example, carbamazepine is the generic name of a medication sold under the brand names Equetro and Tegretol.

Are generic drugs safe?

Generic drugs are usually as good as brand names, but I have worked with patients who clearly did better on brand name medications, which are usually more consistent in potency and are manufactured to higher standards.

Recently, there has been an influx of counterfeit medications made overseas. These are packaged to look like name brand and generic medicines and shipped to the United States from other countries. Doctors are finding that many of these products are out of date, adulterated with filth, or contain the wrong medication. The best protection from counterfeits is to do business with a pharmacist that you personally know and trust.

How long will I have to take these same medications for bipolar disorder?

If medication and research were to remain the same, you would have to take the same bipolar medications for the rest of your life. However, there is an explosion of new treatments for bipolar disorder, and there will be many better medications and nonmedication treatments for bipolar illness available within the next few years.

Can I stop taking mood stabilizers cold turkey?

No. Like most medications, it is better to taper slowly according to your doctor's instructions rather than stopping them suddenly.

Carbamazepine (Equetro, Tegretol, Carbatrol, and Other Brands)

Doctors that work extensively with bipolar disorder all have their favorite mood stabilizer. Overall, my patients have liked taking carbamazepine the best.

In addition to regular tablets, carbamazepine comes in a flavored, chewable tablet. Carbamazepine is also available in a liquid form but it settles out in the bottle and is unsatisfactory unless you remember to shake it aggressively every time you use it.

My stepsister takes carbamazepine for
     epilepsy. Is carbamazepine licensed
     to treat bipolar disorder?

Carbamazepine has been used successfully for years to treat both bipolar disorder and temporal lobe epilepsy (TLE). Equetro is a brand of time-released carbamazepine that is licensed for use in bipolar disorder. The very same medication is licensed for use in TLE under the name of Carbatrol. At this time, most of the brands of carbamazepine are still only licensed for use in seizures. The thing to remember is that all forms contain the same ingredient, carbamazepine.

What symptoms of bipolar disorder will
     carbamazepine improve?

Carbamazepine stabilizes brain cells and treats the central cause of bipolar disorder so it will improve all bipolar symptoms. I especially notice less anger, less anxiety, better logical thought, and more normal sleep patterns in my patients taking carbamazepine.

I read that researchers gave students
     carbamazepine, and it just made them
     sleepy. What does that mean?

Bipolar medications work by normalizing the imbalances of bipolar disorder. If anybody without bipolar disorder took carbamazepine, they would probably feel nothing or perhaps they would feel some mild sedation. Certainly, they would experience no benefits.

How long will I have to wait for results after starting carbamazepine?

I have seen patients who experienced a clear reduction in their bipolar symptoms after only a few days of taking carbamazepine. However, increased benefits are usually seen after the optimum dose has been continued for ten days to three weeks.

What are the side effects of carbamazepine?

It is hard to predict whether you will experience any side effects when you start taking carbamazepine. If you do, side effects may include mild sedation, nausea, fuzzy vision, or dizziness that usually goes away after a few days. Similar symptoms may occur if the carbamazepine dose is too high or if the dose is increased too fast. When carbamazepine is increased gradually, the likelihood of side effects is significantly reduced.

A very small proportion of the population has a deficit in the production of the liver enzyme called CYP-ZD6 that digests carbamazepine. These "slow metabolizers" break down carbamazepine so slowly that carbamazepine backs up in the bloodstream, where it may increase two to ten times the expected blood level. These few people respond as if they are taking an unusually high dose of carbamazepine and may have symptoms like sedation, nausea, dizziness, or fuzzy vision even when they are only taking a small dose. For these people, carbamazepine must be given at very low doses.

Carbamazepine can cause a very small number of people to have a rash, usually in the first few months after starting the medication. In my patients who have been affected, the rash appears as red spots and bumps that are neither itchy nor painful. Pediatricians have told me that this rash looks like the beginning of chicken pox. If this rash persists, it can become severe or even fatal. For this reason, doctors usually tell their patients to stop carbamazepine if they get a rash and either call them or come for an appointment right away. I have prescribed truckloads of carbamazepine in my life and I have only seen the rash in about five patients.

Very rarely, carbamazepine can cause an anemia with loss of blood cells. This anemia could result in fatality if not treated. Working closely with a physician and periodic clinical examination and blood tests can help catch this rare reaction if it occurs.

Carbamazepine can reduce the effectiveness of some birth control pills. Check with your gynecologist or primary care doctor to see if there is any need to adjust these medicines.

After taking carbamazepine for a while, will I have to increase the dose?

Carbamazepine speeds its own metabolism by producing more liver enzymes. After two to six months of treatment, a slight increase in dose may be needed to keep your blood level constant.

I got bipolar disorder after a head injury. Do you recommend carbamazepine for me and why?

Bipolar disorder that occurs after stroke or head injury often responds to carbamazepine.

Can I have sex while I take carbamazepine?

I have never heard of carbamazepine interfering with sexual performance. Several patients I know actually take their carbamazepine before having sex because they feel it relaxes them.

Will carbamazepine work if I have social anxiety disorder?

I often use carbamazepine successfully to treat social anxiety in people who have bipolar disorder.

Oxcarbazepine (Trileptal)

Oxcarbazepine (Trileptal) is a medication that closely resembles carbamazepine at the molecular level. Like carbamazepine, the danger of rash is also present, as is the risk for anemia, although there have been few cases reported to date. Oxcarbazepine is usually managed without blood tests. For these reasons, some clinicians are discarding carbamazepine and starting their bipolar patients on oxcarbazepine instead. I have used oxcarbazepine for a number of patients who had difficulty taking blood tests and it worked satisfactorily. However, research has not yet proved that oxcarbazepine works as well as carbamazepine.

Does oxcarbazepine change your hormones?

There is some evidence that oxcarbazepine causes a mild increase in male hormones. So far, my male patients have been more satisfied with oxcarbazepine than the women.

Is oxcarbazepine licensed to treat bipolar disorder?

Not at this time.

Valproate and Valproic Acid (Depakote and Depakene)

Valproate is a drug that normalizes the rhythm of brain cells and increases the amount of a brain chemical (called gamma-aminobutyric acid or GABA) that is important in brain cell regulation. Valproate also increases the production of certain blood proteins that appear to protect nerve cells from injury and aging. Valproate is licensed to treat bipolar disorder, seizures, migraine headaches, and as an aid to stop smoking cigarettes.

Valproate came along at a time when doctors were starting to question whether lithium salt (discussed later in this chapter) was the only way to treat mania. Studies have shown that valproate is one of the best bipolar medicines. It has been heavily advertised and promoted by pharmaceutical companies and is now a very popular treatment for bipolar illness.

What's the difference between Depakote and Depakene?

Depakote brand regular and extended-release tablets contain both valproate and valproic acid. To save space, I will refer to the active ingredient in Depakote as valproate. Depakote products are covered with a coating that delays absorption of the medicine until it is in the lower digestive tract, which reduces stomach upset.

Depakene capsules and liquid contain only valproic acid, not valproate. They have no coating to reduce stomach cramps and pain. The discomfort associated with Depakene can be considerable for some, so I never prescribe Depakene.

What symptoms of bipolar disorder will valproate improve?

As with other mood stabilizers, valproate treats the central cause of bipolar disorder so that it will improve all bipolar symptoms. In particular, people taking valproate note increased clarity of thinking, fewer obsessional thoughts, and better communication with others. I often notice early improvements in talking too much and too fast.

How does valproate feel when you take it? I don't want anything that'll make me feel weird.

Subjectively, my patients tell me they feel less like they are taking a medication with valproate than with other mood stabilizers. Of course, you can tell you are taking valproate when you see things getting better in your life.

What side effects might I expect
when I start valproate?

Most of my patients have no side effects when they start taking valproate. If they do, the most common experience that I see is a mild sedation that usually goes away in a few days.

Weight gain often appears later in the course of treatment, probably as a result of increased insulin secretion. Hair loss, swollen ankles, and tremor can sometimes appear. There is some evidence that valproate can worsen existing polycystic ovary disease by slightly raising male hormone levels.

Rarely, valproate can cause side effects involving the liver. This usually shows up as a change in the blood tests used to measure liver function. This reaction can sometimes progress to liver failure, so it is important to work closely with your doctor, especially during the first few months of taking valproate. Patients with a history of liver problems might want to consider another medication.

Lithium Salt (Eskalith, Lithobid, and Other Brands)

Lithium salt is the oldest, most reliable medication for bipolar disorder. It is the only one that has been proved effective in doctors' offices and clinical studies around the world for over a century. It is the oldest mood stabilizer, and we have a good idea of how safe it is and how to manage the medication.

Lithium salt formed the basis of many popular health supplements throughout the world during the 1800s. In Europe, lithium salt was formally introduced as a medicine in 1843. After miraculous recoveries were demonstrated in "untreatable" patients, lithium salt became established as the first effective treatment for bipolar mania and depression in 1871.

However, in 1948, lithium salt was introduced in the United States as a substitute for table salt in people suffering from heart problems. When several individuals took enormous quantities of the salt and died, the public was in an uproar. Lithium salt regained popularity for use in bipolar disorder during the 1960s, and it was formally labeled for the treatment of bipolar disorder by the Federal Drug Administration (FDA) in 1970.

Is lithium salt a natural treatment for bipolar depression?

Lithium salt is the only naturally occurring treatment for bipolar disorder. It has long been known as the basis of the healing properties of European spa waters, where it occurs naturally.

How does lithium salt work in the body?

Like other mood stabilizers, lithium salt works to normalize brain cell rhythm. Lithium salt is so much like natural body salts that it can substitute freely throughout the nervous system for sodium and potassium minerals. Lithium salt helps regulate the release of excitatory neurochemicals called noradrenaline and dopamine. It also increases the production of certain blood proteins that appear to protect nerve cells from injury and aging.

Lithium salt is marketed in regular release capsules, delayed release tablets and capsules, and lithium citrate, a flavored lithium syrup.

My wife has bipolar depression, not mania. Will lithium salt help her?

Lithium salt is thought to be one of the best mood stabilizers for relieving bipolar depression symptoms and preventing their reoccurrence. Studies suggest that lithium salt may give extra protection against suicidal behavior.

What are the side effects of lithium salt?

Weight gain is a problem with lithium salt. To keep from gaining weight it is necessary to carefully watch your caloric intake, maintain good nutrition, and get regular aerobic exercise. Most adults need to adopt these practices anyway to keep healthy, whether they are taking lithium salt or not.

Lithium salt can cause some people to experience acne or coarse hair. Some people experience hand tremors. My patients seldom complain of sexual problems when taking lithium salt. However, if your sex drive is abnormally high in mania or abnormally low in depression, it will go back to normal with treatment.

My patients usually describe these side effects as being minor, if they are present at all. However, I have seen more severe problems occur if lithium salt levels have been allowed to go too high or if patients have a history of drinking too much alcohol.

Why am I thirsty when I take lithium salt? And why do I pee so much?

Like table salt, lithium salt can make you thirsty and make you want to drink more fluids. It has additional effects as a diuretic, increasing the volume of urine output.

Although the intake of any salt can make you more thirsty, it is always best to avoid drinking too much fluid while taking lithium salt. Too much water can dilute nutrients needed by the body. As Socrates said, "Moderation in all things."

What can happen if the lithium blood level goes too high?

If the lithium salt in your bloodstream becomes too concentrated for too long a time, it can damage the kidneys. Your doctor will probably prescribe blood tests to make sure the concentration is not too high.

Sometimes lithium salt can become too concentrated if your body loses lots of fluid and you cannot replace it. This can happen during illness because of vomiting, diarrhea, and fever, especially if you cannot retain fluids. If this happens, consult your doctor, who may advise you to skip a dose of medicine or temporarily decrease your dose until you are able to drink liquids again.

How can I replace fluids if I can't keep anything down?

In severe bouts of vomiting and diarrhea in children, doctors recommend taking liquids that are filled with electrolytes and other necessary nutrients. This technique works just as well in adults. The best example of this type of product is called Pedialyte, and you can find it at your local grocery or drugstore. I always keep a bottle in my refrigerator.

Alternatively, you may do what everyone else in the world does and drink rice water. To make rice water, take rice and boil it in plenty of water. When the rice is reduced to a pulpy mush, the soupy liquid that you drain off is rice water.

Can older people take lithium salt even if their kidneys are in bad shape?

Many elders and patients with kidney disease can take lithium salt if they are monitored closely by an experienced physician. In practice, I try not to prescribe lithium salt to people with known kidney problems.

Can lithium salt affect my thyroid gland?

A decrease in the production of thyroid hormone is sometimes seen with lithium salt. Doctors often check the performance of the thyroid by ordering blood tests, such as "TSH," "serum free T4," and "serum free T3."

Can my doctor help manage or reduce the side effects of lithium salt?

There is a lot of art in the management of lithium salt and its side effects. Experienced doctors often have strategies to reduce lithium side effects.

Some of my tricks include starting at low doses, giving the lithium salt once at night, and using time-release lithium salt tablets to smooth out the level of lithium in the blood.

I found mineral water with lithium salt in it. Can I take that? I like mineral water.

I have seen waters and nonprescription tablets said to contain lithium salt. In every case I have investigated, the products did not contain enough lithium salt to be of any use. Moreover, to ensure safety, the dose of lithium salt you take to treat bipolar disorder must be carefully managed by a physician. Given the variations in the amount of lithium salt present in these unregulated products, I advise my patients not to use them.

Do you prescribe a lot of lithium salt? Why or why not?

Lithium salt is a very effective treatment for bipolar disorder. In addition, I sometimes add lithium salt to existing medications to make them work better. However, in the town where I practice medicine, there are many people in the entertainment business who are greatly concerned about their personal appearance for career reasons. They are often hesitant to try any medicine that might cause weight gain, acne, or coarse hair, so they usually start on another mood stabilizer.

Lamotrigine (Lamictal)
Lamotrigine is another mood-stabilizing, antiseizure medication that is an effective treatment for bipolar disorder. Lamotrigine works by blocking glutamate, an important neurotransmitter biochemical in the brain. As a mood stabilizer, Lamictal treats the core pathology of bipolar disorder and so it reduces all bipolar symptoms. In addition, it helps reduce the production of stress hormones.

Lamictal is a good general mood stabilizer that reduces the symptoms of bipolar mania and depression. However, it is not clear that lamotrigine can block a cycle of depression from starting. After bipolar depression has already started, it may be too late to reverse it completely.

Lamotrigine comes in regular and chewable tablets.

How do you decide when to prescribe lamotrigine?

I have had the best luck with lamotrigine when it is added to a major mood stabilizer. It is also useful in individuals who have failed with a major mood stabilizer or who cannot tolerate giving blood for blood tests.

What are the usual side effects of lamotrigine?

One recent study found that the most common side effects after taking lamotrigine were headache and nausea. Those were the same symptoms commonly reported by control patients taking a placebo.

As with some other medicines, some people can get a rash with red bumps and blisters that usually do not hurt or itch. This rash is more prevalent when doses are raised rapidly. If this lamotrigine rash persists, it can become severe or even fatal. For this reason, doctors usually tell their patients to stop lamotrigine if they get a rash and either call or come for an appointment right away.

How do you dose lamotrigine?

Current licensing suggests starting at a low dose and increasing slowly every week. Ever since doctors began to raise lamotrigine doses slowly, there have been few cases of the rash.

Lamotrigine can interact with some other medications to change their levels in the blood. For this reason, doctors are advised to use a lower lamotrigine dose if they are combining lamotrigine with valproate, and to use a higher lamotrigine dose when combining with carbamazepine. Check with your doctor and see what she or he recommends.

Will lamotrigine give me energy?

My patients tell me that lamotrigine is not sedating in any way. Some of them say they have increased activation and more motivation without manic symptoms.

Does lamotrigine cause weight gain?

Unlike carbamazepine, valproate, or lithium salt, lamotrigine does not cause weight gain in my patients. A number of my patients have even lost weight while taking lamotrigine.

Topiramate (Topamax)

Topiramate normalizes brain cell rhythm and stimulates one natural neurochemical that helps regulate brain cell function (gamma-aminobutyric acid) and another that reduces the production of stress hormones (glutamate).

I have had some great successes treating patients with topiramate, particularly for adolescent boys with bipolar disorder and behavior problems. However, some of my patients have not benefited from it and, at this time, I do not know whether topiramate can block manic or depressive cycles from occurring. For these reasons, I seldom use topiramate as the first line of treatment. I am hoping to discover the secret to getting maximum benefits from topiramate so I can use it more often.

Topiramate is available in tablets and capsules that can be opened and sprinkled over food for individuals that cannot take pills. At this time, topiramate is only licensed for the treatment of seizure disorders and migraine headaches.

Can I lose weight by taking topiramate?

Many of my patients have lost weight when taking topiramate. Sometimes I will add it to other mood stabilizers to block weight gain. For example, I was treating a woman whose weight had gradually crept up over the years while taking valproate. When we added topiramate, she began losing up to five pounds per month, which made her happy. We also noticed that her level of irritability was decreased after adding topiramate.

What are the major side effects of topiramate?

Some serious potential side effects listed for topiramate include changes in the acidity of the blood, worsening of glaucoma, decreased sweating, sedation, and kidney stones.

Will topiramate give me more energy?

Many patients tell me that they find topiramate somewhat energizing. No one has ever told me that it made them sleepy.

Gabapentin (Neurontin)

Many doctors like gabapentin (Neurontin) for several reasons. It produces a mild, relaxing feeling in almost everyone. It does not cause significant sedation, insomnia, weight gain, or other bad side effects. It has few drug interactions and a low potential for addiction or overdose. Gabapentin is currently used for the treatment of seizures, migraines, pain, anxiety, and many other things.

In many ways, gabapentin seems to be the ideal medication. However, in my experience, it has not been very helpful in the treatment of bipolar disorder and it is not licensed for that purpose. For some time, there were rumors that it was necessary to increase gabapentin to very high doses in order to get a good effect against bipolar disorder. I have not found this to be true. The only use I have found for gabapentin in bipolar disorder is as an augmenting agent added to other drugs. To date, I have found a handful of patients who benefited from gabapentin used in this way.

Tiagabine (Gabitril)

Tiagabine (Gabitril) is a medication developed for seizure disorders that increases the naturally occurring neurochemical called GABA (gamma-aminobutyric acid) that reduces anxiety. It is being considered as a new treatment for bipolar disorder. However, you should know that there are reports of tiagabine causing seizures in people who never had seizures before. For this reason, I do not use tiagabine at this time.

Levetiracetam (Keppra)

Levetiracetam (Keppra) is a novel medication licensed to reduce seizures. It is not licensed to treat bipolar disorder. At this point, we know little about how levetiracetam works in the body. Patients that have come to me after being given levetiracetam for bipolar disorder have had nothing particularly good to say about it.

ATYPICAL ANTIPSYCHOTICS

Just because a medication comes from a class called "antipsychotic" does not suggest that you are psychotic any more than using medications called anticonvulsants implies that you have epilepsy. The origin of the name antipsychotic goes back to the history of this family of medications when they were mostly used to treat schizophrenia. The newer medications in this class are usually called atypicals because they are different from the older members of the family. I will usually refer to these medications as atypicals.

What kinds of effects can I expect with atypicals?

I have seen atypicals reduce symptoms of mania, depression, irritability, and anxiety. They can improve sleeping, reduce distractibility, and minimize agitation, aggression, and temper tantrums. In bipolar depression, they improve motivation and make it easier to start and finish projects. They can often stop or decrease intrusive, obsessive thoughts.

Are atypicals better or safer than older antipsychotic medicines?

Twenty years ago, antipsychotics were only recommended to treat hallucinations and delusions. However, my mentors told me, "Antipsychotics are great drugs for all phases of bipolar disorder but you will not find this in the books." Now, with the availability of atypicals, everyone is again discovering that these medications are useful in bipolar disorder. Most atypicals are licensed by the Federal Drug Administration (FDA) as treatments for bipolar disorder.

Atypicals affect many neurochemical systems, including the serotonin system. This is one reason why atypicals reduce bipolar depression and mania more than older antipsychotics.

The biggest danger of traditional antipsychotic medicines was their potential to produce movement disorders. These ranged from restless walking to unnatural movements of the face and limbs. The newer atypicals appear to be fairly free from these side effects, and most doctors feel they are safer than the older medications.

Are atypicals as good as mood stabilizers?

In my experience, mood stabilizers work much better than atypicals for the treatment of bipolar disorder. However, atypicals work differently than mood stabilizers (discussed earlier in this chapter), so the two complement each other. I usually start patients on a mood stabilizer first and consider adding an atypical later, if needed.

Can atypicals keep manic and depressive episodes from starting?

Classical mood stabilizers like carbamazepine, valproate, and lithium salt can block mania and depression from starting, which is the primary goal of bipolar treatment. However, this is not always the case with atypicals. In one study, 46 percent of patients treated with only an atypical had another manic episode while on their medication. A 46 percent chance of losing your job, family, friends, money, house, and self respect is not acceptable. When treating my patients, I look for medications that can prevent all manic and depressive episodes from occurring for years at a time.

What is the most popular atypical used to treat bipolar disorder?

In my experience, olanzapine (Zyprexa) is a very effective treatment for bipolar disorder. In fact, it may be the most effective atypical for treating the brain systems responsible for bipolar disorder. However, it is sedating. The worst problem is significant weight gain. This weight gain increases the risk for other health problems, including diabetes. I have used olanzapine successfully for bipolar individuals who were too thin and wanted to return to their natural weight.

What atypical do you currently use the most?

Right now, I am having good results with ziprasidone (Geodon). My patients tell me that it is not sedating and that it does not make them gain weight. It has been helpful in normalizing brain biochemistry to control bipolar depression and mania as well as anxiety and intrusive thoughts. Sometimes it appears to be effective at a relatively low dose. It may increase the chances of heart arrhythmia, so I do not give it in the presence of heart disease.

My usual practice is to establish a mood stabilizer and add Geodon; I do not use it alone or as a first medication. That and the fact that I do not give antidepressants to bipolar patients may improve my success with Geodon.

Is Seroquel an effective treatment?

Quetiapine (Seroquel) has been shown effective in the treatment of bipolar disorder and is licensed for that use. It is fast becoming popular with physicians.

When it is given at bedtime, quetiapine is sedating and can help people get to sleep. However, the sedation is a problem if it carries over into the day. Quetiapine can cause moderate weight gain.

What do you think of clozapine?

Clozapine (Clozaril) was the first atypical, and some studies show that it works better than the others. Many doctors, including myself, do not prescribe it because it can cause blood problems, it is very sedating, and it causes significant weight gain.

How about risperidone?

My bipolar patients have not had very good success with risperidone (Risperdal). It can cause movement disorders, albeit rarely, and several of my patients' mania became worse while taking it. It also causes moderate weight gain.

Do you use Abilify?

I am still waiting for more information and research on the effects of aripiprazole (Abilify) on bipolar disorder before giving it to my bipolar patients. In one study, it caused weight gain in 11 percent of volunteers who took it. It also has the potential to lower the blood pressure slightly, so be careful not to sit or stand up too quickly if you start taking it.

What is the rationale for combining different bipolar medications?

Bipolar patients often need to take more than one type of medication to control their illness adequately. By combining medicines, you can get several types of benefits and possibly keep the dose of each medication low. Traditionally, physicians have combined carbamazepine, valproate, and/or lithium salt in all possible combinations. Now doctors are combining major mood stabilizers with atypical antipsychotics (like ziprasidone) and with newer mood stabilizers (like lamotrigine or topiramate).

ANTIANXIETY MEDICATIONS

Many closely related antianxiety medications are available, including alprazolam (Xanax), lorazepam (Ativan), clonazepam (Klonopin), and diazepam (Valium). Although they are marketed as antianxiety medications, all of them are just general sedatives; they have no specific physiological actions against anxiety. Although they are not licensed for this use, these medications are often given to bipolar patients when they complain of anxiety or panic. However, all they do is sedate you; they never treat the core bipolar problems like mood stabilizers do.

Are sedatives an effective treatment for bipolar disorder?

These medications lower your overall energy level but they do not treat the part of the brain responsible for bipolar disorder. They do not help treat depression, repetitive thoughts, distractibility, or poor memory. Studies have shown that sedatives can make people more irritable and angry even without their realizing it. Sedatives are also addictive, induce withdrawal, and can cause failure of the breathing response if taken in overdose or with alcohol.

I never use sedatives alone or as the main part of my treatment for bipolar disorder. I have seen many bipolar individuals waste away their lives and their talent while taking only sedatives. However, I am convinced that mild doses of sedatives can improve the life quality of some persons with bipolar disorder. If I give sedatives at all, I usually give low doses of Ativan or Klonopin.

SELDOM USED MEDICATIONS THAT CAN HELP BIPOLAR DISORDER

There are a handful of medications which are not found in most bipolar references that experienced clinicians use because they have found them to be useful in bipolar disorder. In many cases, these medications are not promoted by the pharmaceutical companies and are not currently the subject of active research. None of them is specifically labeled for bipolar disorder at this time. If you consider medications from this group, be sure you discuss the possible benefits and risks with your physician.

What is clonidine?

Clonidine (Catapres) is only licensed as a blood pressure medicine. Nevertheless, clonidine is often used for childhood problems of attention and obsessiveness, as well as Tourette's syndrome and tic disorders. It appears to act like a mood stabilizer. Clonidine helps regulate the release of adrenaline in key centers of the brain by turning on specific adrenaline switches located on brain cells (called alpha-2 receptors). It is effective, I believe, because adrenaline is out of control in bipolar disorder. At the right doses, I have also seen clonidine reduce anger and anxiety in bipolar disorder. Clonidine can improve bipolar symptoms if patients are not yet ready to take a stronger mood stabilizer.

Clonidine can be a good starting point for bipolar treatment in some patients. Clonidine is fairly safe and comes in tiny pills that are easy to take. In addition to pills, clonidine is available in the form of an adhesive patch that is applied to the skin and changed every week. The patch can be a more comfortable method of administering the medication, especially for those who are uncomfortable taking pills.

Years ago, I worked with a group of homeless people with bipolar disorder who were so paranoid that they had never taken any medications of any kind. They would not take a pill, but many of them would wear a clonidine patch. In many cases, clonidine decreased their symptoms so much that they could function better and would tolerate oral mood stabilizers.

Clonidine tablets are frequently taken once at bedtime because they usually make people quite sleepy for several hours after they are taken. Thus, clonidine can also be helpful in insomnia caused by bipolar disorder.

What are monoamine oxidase inhibitors (MAOIs)?

Monoamine Oxidase Inhibitors (MAOIs) were the first medications that were useful for depression, anxiety disorders, anger episodes, and other emotional disorders. Despite the increasing popularity of newer drugs to treat these conditions, many physicians, including myself, believe that MAOIs are still the best available treatment for depression and anxiety disorders. Because MAOIs are not new, there is no profit to be made from them, meaning that drug companies do not even advertise them and doctors are prescribing them less often. MAOIs are licensed for the treatment of depression, including bipolar depression. There are several brands of MAOIs available. My experience is that each brand of MAOI works differently in bipolar disorder.

What are the side effects of MAOIs?

When MAOIs are mistakenly taken with certain drugs and foods, they can cause an increase in blood pressure, which, if not treated, could be severe or fatal. Your doctor can provide you with a list of the items you must avoid. They include over-the-counter decongestants and fermented foods such as beer, wine, fermented vinegar, and aged cheeses. Let your other doctors and dentist know you are taking an MAOI so they can make sure that you do not get any prescription drugs that could interact with your antidepressant.

No one should be placed on MAOIs unless they can be trusted to take them exactly as prescribed and reliably stay on the diet. Most of my patients comment on how easy it is to follow the diet, which contains lots of things that they never ate anyway.

I also give my patients a pill that can rapidly reverse high blood pressure to keep with them at all times. Over the past twenty years, only four or five of my patients have ever needed to take it.

What is Parnate? Is it any good for bipolar depression?

The MAOI called tranylcypromine (Parnate) is very effective against bipolar depression, and I have never seen it cause mania in my patients. It is surely one of the best treatments for bipolar depression. However, tranylcypromine must be reserved for people who are able to monitor their own behavior, follow the rules, and maintain a good therapeutic relationship with their psychiatrist. In the right people and the right situations, tranylcypromine can work wonders for bipolar depression, anxiety, anger, and obsessive thoughts.

Are there side effects from Parnate?

Minor side effects from tranylcypromine are variable and, if they occur at all, are usually gone after a month. The most common side effect is temporary low blood pressure. To prevent complications due to low blood pressure, it is important not to stand up quickly. Instead, wait a minute and steady yourself before you rise from bed, get out of a chair, or bend over. It also helps to eat more salt temporarily. I recommend salted cashews and tomato juice.

Occasionally, patients will complain of sedation with tranylcypromine. This is probably because the feedback system that controls noradrenaline has kicked in. I have had good luck making this sedation go away by supplementing with the amino acid called tyrosine.

Is phenylzine an effective treatment for bipolar?

I have often seen the MAOI called phenelzine (Nardil) trigger severe mania and/or psychosis, and I do not recommend it.

Unfortunately, almost all the research on MAOIs has been done on phenelzine, and little has been done on tranylcypromine. Most of the side effects of "MAOIs" listed in books and on the Internet are those of phenelzine, not tranylcypromine. For example, weight gain is listed as a common side effect of MAOIs, but my experience has revealed that this occurs with phenelzine but not with tranylcypromine. My patients also report sexual side effects with phenelzine but not with tranylcypromine; and phenelzine is sedating but tranylcypromine is often activating. And of course, phenelzine triggers mania.

My friend takes Cytomel. What is that?

Cytomel, also called liothyronine, is a thyroid replacement that is mainly used when the thyroid gland produces too little hormone. Research has shown that bipolar depression may improve when Cytomel is added to other bipolar medications.

Most doctors are more familiar with another thyroid supplement called thyroxine (Synthroid) than they are with Cytomel. Thyroxine is appropriate to treat thyroid disease but it is not very effective for bipolar disorder, so you may need to find a doctor who is knowledgeable about both bipolar disorder and the use of Cytomel to guide you on its use.

Are there heart medicines that might help bipolar disorder?

There is a family of medications called calcium-channel blockers that include verapamil (Isoptin), diltiazem (Cardizem), and nifedipine (Procardia). These medications work by changing the way electrical charges pass through nerve cells. They are licensed for use in high blood pressure, heart problems, and headaches, including migraines. Calcium-channel blockers also have mood-stabilizing properties. I have used them to supplement major mood stabilizers when other medications were not effective or were not tolerated. For example, I knew a woman who had only partial relief of her bipolar symptoms with valproate and took the calcium-channel blocker verapamil to relieve the rest. Calcium-channel blockers are not licensed for bipolar disorder.

NEW MEDICATIONS FOR BIPOLAR DISORDER

We are still learning about the properties and uses of these medicines. With the exception of lamotrigine, none has been licensed for use in bipolar disorder yet.

What are steroids? Do they make bipolar disorder worse?

Steroids are natural stress hormones that the body produces in the course of daily life. They are manufactured for medical use in the treatment of severe infections, cancer, and musculoskeletal injuries. Steroids are known to cause depression and psychosis, particularly in persons with bipolar disorder.

Small doses of steroids are also used to decrease inflammation, like those injected into joints after injury. Some persons with bipolar disorder can tolerate these small doses, while others find that these injections increase their bipolar symptoms.

So-called "natural steroids" are usually extracted from plants. I have seen severe depression and suicidal thoughts follow the use of these products by persons with bipolar disorder.

Since stress steroids make bipolar disorder worse, would blocking them make me feel better?

That is a good question and researchers are working on the answer right now. I believe that steroid-blocking drugs are potentially a great new treatment for bipolar disorder and may significantly reduce the symptoms of both mania and bipolar depression. Antalarmin is one new drug that blocks the body's response to stress. It works by down-regulating the brain areas that signal the body to produce body stress steroids (the hypothalamus and pituitary). With no signal to produce them, the body stops manufacturing stress steroids and the physical response to stress decreases. I look forward to seeing how this research progresses.

Can't you block the glands that secrete body stress steroids?

Body stress hormones like cortisol are released by the adrenal glands, which are located on top of the kidneys. Mifepristone (Mifeprex) reduces excess body steroid hormones caused by overstimulation of the adrenal glands. It does this by turning off the switches (glucocorticoid receptors) in the adrenal glands that turn stress steroids on. Studies are in progress now to see if this approach will normalize brain physiology in bipolar disorder.

I heard that some drug for Alzheimer's can
treat depression. What's the scoop?

Memantine (Namenda) is licensed for the treatment of Alzheimer's de-
mentia. It regulates nerve cells that produce a biochemical called glutamate,
which helps control the body's production of stress steroids. The National
Institute of Mental Health (NIMH) is currently studying how this drug
could be used for depression.

I heard there are mood stabilizers that block
stress steroids. What are they?

Lamotrigine (Lamictal) and topiramate (Topamax) block glutamate, which
plays a role in the release of body steroid hormones. Therefore, these mood
stabilizers may be particularly effective for bipolar depression.

My friend with ALS said she felt less
depressed taking a drug called riluzole.
Could that possibly help my bipolar
depression?

Riluzole (Rilutek) is a drug used to treat amyotrophic lateral sclerosis (ALS)
that also blocks glutamate. It is being investigated to see if it will reduce depression.

Are there any new antiseizure medicines that
could help bipolar sufferers?

Because mood stabilizers also block seizures, every new anticonvulsant is
evaluated to see if it might help bipolar disorder. Pregabalin (Lyrica) is one
such medication that appears to reduce anxiety and is currently under investigation.

Is there some antinausea drug that can also reduce depression?

Aprepitant (Emend) blocks a pain-producing hormone called Substance P. This medication may reduce the brain cell stress damage in the area of the brain that controls the production of body stress steroids (the hypothalamus) and therefore it might help control bipolar depression.

Have you heard about this drug Modafinil?

Modafinil has been licensed to treat certain sleep disorders. Researchers think that it works on the histamine neurochemical system and is different from other available stimulants. I have tried using it as a last resort for short-term relief of fatigue in bipolar depression. However, we do not yet know for sure whether it is safe to use in bipolar disorder without triggering mania or depression.

TREATMENTS FOR BIPOLAR DISORDER THAT DO NOT USE MEDICATIONS

I am always asked if there are medical treatments for bipolar disorder that do not involve medications. In fact, there are definitely some new treatments that hold promise for improving bipolar disorder. Bear in mind that our knowledge of these techniques is still limited and, unlike medications, none of them has been proven capable of blocking bipolar episodes from occurring in the first place.

Magnetic Resonance Imaging

On January 1, 2004, a paper from Harvard University was published describing a kind of brain scan that improved mood in persons with bipolar disorder. Usually brain scans are tools for discovering injuries in the brain. Magnetic Resonance Imaging (MRI) is a technique where a patient is placed inside a huge, powerful, round magnet. Computers analyze the body's magnetic field to provide an image of the structures inside the body. MRIs are frequently used in hospitals to help diagnose medical problems.

One type of MRI, called Echo Planer Magnetic Resonance Spectro-scopic Imaging (EP-MRSI), is used to construct a three-dimensional image of the brain and body. Doctors using this kind of scan were surprised to find that some of their patients reported feeling happier after being scanned. To test this, researchers gave EP-MRSI scans to thirty people with bipolar disorder and then gave them a questionnaire to rate their mood. Twenty-three of the thirty patients (78 percent) reported feeling happier after the scan. Changes in mood occurred immediately after the scan and lasted from hours to days. Further study of this effect is now under way.

This provocative study leaves many important questions unanswered. To find out the truth, we need a study where patients are unequivocally diagnosed as bipolar by experts and are evaluated on validated clinical tests that can measure the severity of bipolar symptoms. Now we merely know that a group of patients who were scanned reported being happier.

Is EP-MRSI safe for me to use?

Occasional MRIs are usually considered to be harmless and they are certainly safer than other types of scans that employ X-rays. However, we do not know about the safety of repeated EP-MRSI for general health or for bipolar illness. Possible long-term side effects include making bipolar disorder worse or shifting bipolar disorder from depression to a manic stage.

Where can I get an EP-MRSI scan for bipolar disorder?

At present, the only way to receive an EP-MRSI scan for bipolar disorder is by participating in a federally approved research trial. Try inquiring about EP-MRSI research trials at a hospital that is associated with a major university or look on the Internet. Please note that these research trials are to discover if a treatment is safe and effective, which means that this treatment is not known to be safe or effective at this time. The FDA does not license EP-MRSI as an accepted treatment for bipolar disorder, so there is no assurance that the technique is a good one.

Transcranial Magnetic Stimulation

There is now a technology under investigation called repetitive Transcranial Magnetic Stimulation (rTMS). rTMS uses a coil that can be pulsed with a powerful electrical current to create a series of ultra-strong magnetic pulses. The duration of the pulses is so brief that they are measured in microseconds. This technique was developed in the 1980s to test the integrity of nerves in the body. Recently there has been some evidence that treatment with this coil apparatus can affect mood disorders.

In rTMS, patients sit in a chair and hold a saucer-sized coil on their heads while the doctor controls an electric power supply. The apparatus causes rapid pulses of magnetic stimulation to go through the area of the head beneath the coil. Typically, a series of pulses are applied for about twenty minutes. There is no interruption of consciousness and there is no need for anesthesia or sedation. Some people experience a slightly painful sensation on the head but there is no sense of electrical stimulation. One study reported that 8 percent of patients felt headache after the treatment.

Doctors are trying a variety of schedules for giving rTMS and there is no agreement on how many treatments to give or how frequently to give them. One approach is to give a twenty-minute treatment daily for two to three weeks and then stop to observe how much progress has been made. We do not know how long one series of treatments will keep away depression. Perhaps periodic booster treatments will be needed to protect against depression's recurrence.

What's going on in rTMS? How does it really work?

We still have much to learn about the way rTMS works. Originally, doctors speculated that the magnetism acted on magnetic molecules located inside the brain, such as the iron found in red blood cells. Other research has shown changes in brain activity and hormone levels after treatment and these may partially explain the rTMS effect. A more recent theory is that the brief magnetic field increases the electrical field of brain cells, causing them to turn on together momentarily. The synchronous firing of brain cells is thought to alleviate depression.

Does rTMS really work for bipolar disorder?

There is mixed evidence on how rapidly rTMS treatments can reverse depression. Many early studies reported that depression could be reversed just hours after the rTMS treatment was received. More recent, better-controlled studies indicate that the antidepressant effect reaches its peak about two weeks from the first treatment.

Although there are ongoing studies of rTMS in bipolar disorder, most of the studies to date have been focused on depressed mood symptoms and not the entire spectrum of bipolar symptoms. When I checked thirty studies of rTMS, eight of the studies mixed unipolar and bipolar patients together so that it was not possible to determine the effects of rTMS on bipolar disorder alone. Two studies treating mania showed no benefit or worsening of mania after rTMS. I have not found any convincing evidence that rTMS can keep new bipolar episodes from returning. I hope that research doctors in this field will do the necessary studies to clarify the effects of rTMS on core bipolar symptoms.

How do I know that rTMS is safe?

rTMS is not yet licensed as a safe and effective medical treatment for bipolar disorder. This means that the federal government has not concluded that the procedure should be used except under controlled research trials. Many legitimate doctors are not willing to use unlicensed or experimental treatments and, under certain circumstances, such use might be considered unethical. Remember that anyone can buy or build a machine and call it rTMS. It is no small thing to mess with high voltage electricity around the head. In uneducated or inexperienced hands, powerful electricity and magnetism can be dangerous or fatal. I would advise caution in using rTMS at this time. If you are interested in rTMS, look for a federally approved clinical trial at a major university hospital where doctors can explain all the potential risks and benefits.

Q I went to an adviser who applied magnets to my head and sold me some shoes with magnets in them. Will these work like rTMS?

Weak magnets applied to the body or secreted in clothing have been sold in the United States since the Civil War. I have never known anyone who showed any benefit from this type of treatment. Other than the name "magnet," there is no similarity between the strong, high-voltage, pulsed electromagnet used in rTMS and the weak static magnets that are applied to the body. These weak magnets may be good for holding pictures on your refrigerator, but they probably will not improve your health.

Vagus Nerve Stimulation

Vagus Nerve Stimulation (VNS) is a promising but little-known treatment for bipolar disorder. It works like a cardiac pacemaker except that it has contact with the nervous system instead of the heart.

VNS has been used as a treatment for severe epilepsy in the United States since 1997. Doctors found that electrical stimulation of the vagus nerve in the neck could reduce seizures in patients with epilepsy. Some depressed epileptics that received this treatment also noted that their depression was improved as well. Doctors repeated VNS treatment in depressed individuals who did not suffer from seizures and found that VNS could reduce depression in persons without epilepsy, too. This was the first indication that VNS was a potential treatment for depression.

To implant the VNS unit, the patient is put under anesthesia while a surgeon makes an incision in the skin on the front of the chest and inserts a pacemaker the size and shape of a pocket watch. This is anchored in place under the skin of the chest. Wires that lead out of the pacemaker are passed under the skin to the neck, where they are wrapped around a segment of the vagus nerve. The pacemaker delivers tiny pulses of electric stimulation to the vagus nerve at predetermined intervals throughout the day. Like a heart pacemaker, the pulses can be adjusted and the unit can be turned on or off from outside the body. This procedure takes about an hour and it can be done in a doctor's office under local anesthesia.

Doctors do not yet understand exactly what VNS does in the nervous system when it is treating depression. It is known that VNS, like antidepressant medicines, increases the amounts of brain chemicals that are involved in depression, such as serotonin, norepinephrine, gamma-aminobutyric acid (GABA), and glutamate. Increasing these brain chemicals is one way that VNS could relieve depression. VNS also increases the blood flow to some brain areas, particularly in the right side of the brain, and this may contribute to the antidepressant effect of VNS. In addition, VNS has an anti-seizure effect, as do most of the other nonmedical treatments and medications used to treat bipolar disorder.

Does VNS work?

VNS treatments are effective in reducing or eliminating depression in about half of the patients that receive the treatment. This may not sound high, but remember that patients scheduled for VNS treatment have depression that is so severe that other methods of treatment have been ineffective. Another advantage of VNS is that depression relief continues as long as the device is in place. This means that a one-time surgical procedure could potentially eliminate depression for life. There may be other positive effects of VNS as well. For example, some research studies have found that the speed and organization of thoughts may be increased after treatment with VNS.

Are there side effects to VNS?

Individuals with VNS implants usually feel a tickle during the moments that the electrical stimulation is being applied. This sensation usually becomes unnoticeable after a short time. Some studies of VNS in epilepsy have found that less than 1 percent of patients experience surgical complications. Recipients of the pacemaker sometimes report hoarseness, cough, sore throat, or shortness of breath, but these are usually described as minor.

Some studies have found that hypomania, agitation, and/or panic can be induced by VNS treatment. This raises my concern that VNS may be just another procedure that can switch bipolar depression into mania, rather than a true treatment for the core symptoms of bipolar depression. Such switches only exacerbate bipolar disease and may have the potential to permanently worsen bipolar symptoms and decrease the response of the illness to other treatments.

Unfortunately for those with bipolar disorder, most of the research into

VNS for depression does not separate test subjects with bipolar depression from those with the wholly different illness of unipolar major depression. When patient groups are mixed, it becomes difficult to determine the effect of VNS on bipolar disorder alone. We can only hope that, with increasing education about the nature of bipolar disorder, more medical researchers will stop lumping together research subjects who have different disorders and calling them all "depression."

We are also still missing important information necessary to compare the effectiveness of VNS treatment to medication treatment in bipolar disorder. For the average person with bipolar illness, there are already medications that provide good treatment for bipolar mania and depression with minimal side effects. These medications can also prevent bipolar disorder symptoms from recurring after they have been stopped. We do not know if VNS can perform as well at these tasks. In addition, we do not know if VNS alone is enough to treat bipolar disorder or if supplemental medications will also be needed.

I like to live dangerously. Should I get one of these new VNS pacemakers?

VNS is licensed to treat severe depression that cannot be treated by any other means. VNS is not specifically licensed for the treatment of bipolar disorder. At this time, we do not know whether VNS would be effective in treating bipolar disorder nor what its potential risks might be. If you are anxious to try VNS, consider entering a federally approved clinical research trial. These studies are obligated to inform you of all the known risks and potential benefits of the treatment before you participate. Otherwise, I think it is too soon to rush into VNS, even if you can find individual practitioners who are willing to perform the procedure. Be patient and wait until we know more about VNS.

Electro- and Magnetic-Convulsive Therapies

Convulsive therapies provide another example of the mysterious connection between epilepsy and bipolar disorder. We have known since the 1930s that even a minor seizure can almost immediately reduce or eliminate depression and mania.

In electro-convulsive therapy (ECT), a battery-sized electrical stimulation is used to cause a minor seizure in the anesthetized patient. The seizure is so small that the only evidence it has occurred is a slight movement of the big toe, but it is enough to change the course of mood disorders.

Electro-convulsive therapy is the only federally approved, licensed, medication-free treatment that is known to stop both depression and mania and to reduce the risk of their reoccurrence. It can bring about dramatic improvement in depression and mania within minutes to hours after the procedure. Many studies indicate that ECT can be more effective than medications with fewer side effects. Other studies indicate that ECT is so safe that it can even be used to treat pregnant mothers without creating problems for their unborn children.

Recently, a similar type of treatment is being tested that uses magnetic rather than electrical stimulation. Like rTMS, a powerful magnet is placed on the scalp, but in this case, the magnetic pulse triggers a minor seizure. These magnetic treatments may provide some of the benefits of ECT without concerns over direct electrical stimulation.

There is a public controversy surrounding ECT. Patients have told me of bad outcomes they heard about in the popular press. I have even been in communities where the city government made it illegal for doctors to perform ECT, effectively taking away patients' choice of their own health care. I was not around during the abuses of the procedure in the mid-1960s, and I have no direct information about them. I do have direct experience caring for patients after other doctors have given them ECT, and I found that their bipolar symptoms were improved after the procedure.

I do not now nor have I ever offered ECT to my patients. I do not think that I ever will. Currently, it brings with it too much emotional baggage that can come between my patients and me. Even my insurance company requires me to pay an extra fee if I offer ECT. I do discuss ECT with my patients in as much detail as they wish. If a patient believes that they need ECT, I am willing to help them locate a doctor who will perform this treatment for them. I will wait to see the results of research on magnetic convulsive therapy before I make up my mind about that.

MEDICATIONS THAT CAN MAKE
BIPOLAR DISORDER WORSE

Individuals who have bipolar disorder have a unique nervous system physiology. However, pharmaceutical companies and the FDA do not test medications to see if they are safe and effective for people with bipolar dis-

THE DRAMATIC EFFECT OF SEIZURES
ON DEPRESSION

· · · · · ·

One weekend I was working at a major Veterans Administration Medical Center when I received an urgent call from one of the mental health units. A unit nurse asked me to come quickly because a patient was having a seizure. This patient had suffered from epilepsy since childhood. He was known to periodically forget his medicine and have unexpected seizures. He had been admitted to the hospital because of a severe suicidal depression.

I ran down the corridors and entered the ward, where the patient in question was lying on the floor, still twitching. When I bent over to ask him if he was okay, he looked up dreamily and said, "Yes, I guess." A moment later he sat bolt upright with a smile on his face. In a loud voice he said, "I'm all right, and I'm completely over my depression! I'm ready to go home!"

As expected, the patient's seizure had such a potent antidepressant effect that the entire spectrum of his depressive symptoms lifted a few moments after the seizure, and he felt like himself again. I gave him a careful examination that convinced me his depression was truly over, and I sent him home to his relieved family that same evening.

order. Consequently, we do not have good research information about which medications are safe and which you should avoid. I did a search of the *Physicians' Desk Reference* (PDR), and I found many medications that listed side effects of manic behavior or euphoria. Many of the medications on the list were antidepressants, steroids, narcotic pain medicines, migraine medications, stimulants, and antiviral medicines. Many of them can also cause seizures as a side effect.

Antidepressants

Antidepressants are designed and marketed for people with unipolar major depression, an illness that is completely different from bipolar depression. The two conditions present different symptoms, have different biochemistry, and occupy different locations in the brain. Moreover, tests to establish the safety of antidepressants are mostly performed on people with unipolar major depression, so they may not apply to you.

Can't I take antidepressants for my bipolar depression?

I try not to prescribe my bipolar patients medicines in the "antidepressant" class because these medications may not help bipolar depression. If anything, antidepressants can worsen bipolar depression or trigger mania and psychosis. In fact, if you look in the most common physicians' reference, the *Physicians' Desk Reference* (PDR), you will find a warning about triggering mania or worsening bipolar disorder in the documentation for most antidepressants.

Many doctors believe that the increased number and severity of bipolar cases in recent years was caused by giving antidepressants to children who have bipolar depression. We now think that giving antidepressants in childhood made their bipolar disorder more severe for the rest of their lives.

In my practice, I have seen worsened depression, mania, and/or psychosis triggered by normal doses of an array of antidepressants including fluoxetine (Prozac), citalopram (Celexa), fluvoxamine (Luvox), buproprion (Wellbutrin), desipramine (Norpramin), imipramine (Tofranil), protriptaline (Vivactil), amitriptaline (Elavil), and phenylzine (Nardil). At high doses, I have seen mania triggered by paroxetine (Paxil), sertraline (Zoloft), venlafaxine (Effexor), and doxepin (Sinequan).

For example, a normally gentle bipolar woman mistakenly given the antidepressant citalopram (Celexa) began picking physical fights with strangers in public places that were so severe that the police were called; a middle-aged bipolar businessman who was given phenylzine (Nardil) felt so invincible that he had an automobile accident while driving at one hundred miles per hour; a bipolar woman given fluoxetine (Prozac) told everyone off at her prestigious job, cleaned out her family's bank account, and disappeared.

Are there any antidepressants that don't cause mania?

I have never seen trazodone (Desyrel) cause mania or worsen bipolar depression. I have seen trazodone improve sleep and reduce anxiety and anger in persons with bipolar disorder. However, it is still an antidepressant, and I cannot vouch for its safety.

Is it true that you can take antidepressants safely as long as you take another medication, too?

This is currently debated among doctors. Many doctors believe that they can give an antidepressant safely if they combine it with a mood stabilizer or an atypical antipsychotic. There is even a combination medication containing fluoxetine and the antipsychotic olanzapine.

Some studies claim that taking combination treatments is safe because the rate of triggering mania is only around 5 percent. Let's examine that conclusion a little more closely. A 5 percent chance of mania or psychosis is still a one in twenty possibility that you will go to the hospital, lose your savings, break up your family, or destroy your career. I feel that this is too great a chance of potentially ruinous danger.

Keeping bipolar episodes from ever starting in the first place is the most important goal in the treatment of bipolar disorder. I suspect that taking antidepressants can make it harder to block new episodes of bipolar mania, depression, or psychosis. When there are already safe medications available that treat bipolar depression such as mood stabilizers, atypical antipsychotics, the MAOI tranylcypromine (Parnate), and others, why take chances with antidepressants until these questions are resolved?

Do you know of any studies that concluded that antidepressants were safe in bipolar disorder?

One metastudy evaluated many people with bipolar disorder taking antidepressants. Seventy-five percent were taking mood stabilizers of some type at unknown doses. The study length varied from four to ten weeks. The metastudy found that slightly more than 5 percent of bipolar patients receiving antidepressants experienced significant manic episodes. Other research studies I have seen to date show antidepressants triggering mania and psychosis in 5 to 20 percent of persons taking them.

However, these results are misleading because they only count the people who had clearly diagnosable mania during the time of the study. Many antidepressant reactions were not counted in the study. For example, the study did not count people who developed mania that was too mild to diagnose but still interfered with their lives; those whose depression worsened or who developed nonmanic psychosis; those who became more depressed, manic, or psychotic after the study was over, or anyone whose bipolar disorder became more severe and more difficult to treat for the rest of their lives as a result of taking antidepressants. If these additional factors are taken into consideration, I believe that antidepressants harm the lives of people with bipolar disorder at a rate that is much higher than 5 percent.

Are all doctors as concerned as you are about giving antidepressants to people with bipolar disorder?

No. Many doctors believe they can prescribe antidepressants effectively and safely in bipolar disorder, especially in combination with a mood stabilizer. If your doctor wants to give you antidepressants, make sure you understand and agree with the risks.

I took an antidepressant that helped. Why did it stop working?

Antidepressants are not designed to treat bipolar depression, so whether they work and how long they work is unpredictable. When a new patient comes in and lists all the antidepressants they have taken that did not work or stopped working, I immediately suspect bipolar disorder.

Infrequently, when a person with bipolar depression takes an antidepressant, they enjoy a brief burst of mania that lasts from a few days to a few months. Sometimes the manic person does not realize that there is something wrong because it seems sensible that taking an antidepressant could make him or her feel better than ever before.

I have met many individuals who had this brief, ecstatic manic episode and then spent much of their lives "chasing a high," trying to re-create that experience. If their euphoria was triggered by an antidepressant, they may spend years seeing doctors and trying different antidepressants in an attempt to get back to that manic place.

A doctor told me that Wellbutrin would not cause mania. Is that true?

Whenever a new antidepressant medication comes out, doctors all hope that *it* will be the one that is safe to use with bipolar disorder. Unfortunately, I have seen people with bipolar disorder become manic or psychotic when given bupropion (Wellbutrin) at the usual clinical doses.

Years ago, I gave bupropion to a withdrawn seventy-four-year-old grandfather that I did not know had bipolar depression. His mood improved but he became obsessed with oral sex and talked incessantly about it in the presence of his wife, their children, and their neighbors. After I discontinued the buproprion and the poor man returned to normal, his elderly wife came to my office and gave me a piece of her mind.

Narcotics and Pain Relievers

Narcotic pain medicine can make bipolar symptoms worse. For example, I worked with a meticulously careful bipolar man who was given a few Vicodin (hydrocodone and acetaminophen) tablets after minor surgery. In the following days, he became very distractible, his thought process and reactions slowed, and he subsequently had a serious motor vehicle accident. I have also heard many reports from bipolar patients who had psychotic symptoms after taking the narcotic pain medicine called meperidine (Demerol).

In addition to Vicodin and Demerol, I tend to avoid the following brands: Demerol, Dilaudid, Darvocet, Darvon, Lortab, Norco, OxyContin, Percocet, Percodan, Vicoprofen, and Zydone.

Are people with bipolar disorder more likely to be addicted to painkillers?

People with bipolar disorder are inordinately prone to substance abuse, perhaps because many abused substances release mania. In particular, individuals with bipolar illness are at a great risk for narcotic addiction. It's another good reason not to take narcotics in any form.

Is plain codeine okay?

I have seen codeine used safely in bipolar disorder and you may want to try it for pain under a doctor's supervision. However, it may be a moot point because many of my bipolar patients tell me they do not get satisfactory pain relief from codeine.

Could any over-the-counter medications contain narcotics?

They could. Dextromethorphan is a narcotic ingredient found in twelve-hour cough syrup and lozenges. Dextromethorphan is similar to the narcotic meperidine (Demerol), but it does not relieve pain nor is it addictive to people without the disorder. However, I have seen cough syrup containing dextromethorphan trigger severe mania and psychosis.

I once cared for an elderly man who rented apartments and had a very stable life. When he developed a bad cold one winter, he began taking large doses of cough medicine containing dextromethorphan. He subsequently developed his first episode of full-blown psychotic mania. He imagined that a freshman college student who rented one of his apartments had fallen madly in love with him and wanted to write a biography telling the world how wonderful he was. Believing that she wanted to marry him, he spent hours trying to push his affections on the poor young woman. Finally, the man was hospitalized, the cough medicine was stopped, and he was placed on a mood stabilizer. When he became lucid again, he felt very embarrassed, and the college student felt very relieved.

My bipolar patients have had good results with a prescription cough medication called Tessalon Perles (benzonatate) and with a diphenhydramine cough syrup, which you can buy in the drugstore. However, the latter makes many people drowsy. Another alternative is to use an anesthetic throat spray containing phenol (like Chloraseptic) for mild coughs.

Is Fiorinal really a painkiller? My doctor says
     there's no way she'll give it to me anyway.

Technically, butalbital (Fiorinal, Fioricet, Medigesic, Esgic, and Sedapap) is
only a sedative barbiturate, but it does seem to have pain-relieving effects in
many of my bipolar patients. However, it is such a dangerous and addictive
substance that I seldom use it, and I never prescribe more than one day's
worth at a time.

Are there any treatments for pain that don't
     involve taking medicine?

Relaxation and meditation can decrease pain (see chapter 2). There is also a
place for chiropractic and acupuncture for the relief of pain, particularly in
musculoskeletal problems. A process called TENS, which involves the stimulation of pain nerves by mild electrical shocks on the skin, is often effective for
body pain. However, to get the most out of it, you will need to find a practitioner who understands how it works and who is practiced in the technique.

Why do I get sick with bipolar disorder when
     I go to the dentist? Is it the Novocain?

The main offender is probably the adrenaline (also called epinephrine) that
the dentist adds to the local anesthetic to decrease bleeding. Dentists call
this "Novocain with EPI" (pronounced eh'-pee). I believe that abnormal
production of adrenaline is one contributor to the symptoms of bipolar
disorder. When more adrenaline is added to the body, it can throw everything off balance.

4.

How to Find the
Right Doctor

. . . .

In the ideal professional working relationship, a doctor informs his or her patients of the benefits and risks of the best treatment options, and they discuss their concerns together until both agree with the next step. This way, two minds are harnessed to solve each problem. It takes work and the right people to build this trusting relationship.

Which doctors receive training in bipolar medications?

Any doctor can prescribe medications, but psychiatrists have received extensive training in the diagnosis and treatment of mental and emotional disorders. Some psychiatrists (psychopharmacologists) only specialize in medications. Other psychiatrists have a special interest and experience in treating bipolar disorder through medications *and* psychotherapy.

Q I need to find a good psychiatrist. How do I go about locating one?

Ask your current doctors if they know any psychiatrists that they feel comfortable recommending. Look to hospitals associated with major universities to find some of the best doctors in the area. Talk to your local or state medical and psychiatric associations for referrals. If any of your friends have psychiatrists that they like, ask about them. You can also find out about well-liked psychiatrists by attending local meetings and seminars on bipolar disorder and by going to bipolar support groups.

Q What do I need to know about a psychiatrist before I decide to seek treatment with him or her?

Call your state's Board of Medical Quality (or its equivalent) or locate their website online. Confirm that your prospective psychiatrist has a valid license to practice medicine in your state and find out if their license has ever been suspended or revoked. Many states will tell you if doctors are under investigation for malpractice or misconduct charges. Beyond this, you can also choose to research a doctor's credentials by finding out:

- Where they went to school and where they received their psychiatry training
- Whether they have been certified by the board of psychiatry and if they have chosen to be certified by other boards (such as suicidology or geriatric psychiatry)
- Whether they are or have been faculty at any universities and whether their positions were in teaching, research, or clinical areas
- Whether they are members of major medical societies like the American Medical Association (AMA) or the American Psychiatric Association (APA)
- If they have won awards or special recognition

However, there is a problem with this approach. Great credentials are not a sure sign of a great doctor, and some (particularly older) doctors may have wisdom that schooling cannot teach. You cannot find these things out by research.

I suggest that you call up the psychiatrist you are considering and talk with him or her about who they are and what they do. Ask questions that will help you determine whether their background, approach, and personality are what you are looking for, such as:

- Are they interested in treating bipolar disorder?
- Do they feel comfortable prescribing bipolar medications?
- How many bipolar patients are they treating now?
- How many bipolar patients have they treated during their career?
- If you want your psychiatrist to also be your psychotherapist, ask what kinds of therapy they offer and what specific types of therapy they believe are most helpful for bipolar disorder.

Remember that busy professionals may not budget much time to talk to nonpatients, so you may have to be persistent and understanding of other demands on their time.

When you are satisfied, schedule an evaluation appointment, and expect to pay for it. You may wish to take this book along to your appointment to help remember what you want to ask and tell the doctor.

Can a psychiatrist give me more information about bipolar disorder?

A significant portion of the time you spend with your psychiatrist should be spent learning about the illness of bipolar disorder and its treatment. You need to know everything about your illness in order to keep healthy and help direct your own treatment. You will want to find a psychiatrist who is interested and willing to take the time to educate you about your bipolar illness.

Can I find a good doctor in my area?

There are parts of the country where there are very few psychiatrists. If you live in such an area, you may have to choose between a less experienced doctor that you know or driving a long distance to meet with a top-notch specialist who is initially a stranger.

What if the doctor I want to see has a long waiting list, or I can't get an appointment?

If you cannot get in to see a psychiatrist, try asking another doctor to call that psychiatrist and recommend you as a patient. You may also be able to get your family's or friends' doctors to call and recommend you. Be flexible about taking available appointment times or waiting for cancellations.

Can I ask a specialist to meet with me once or twice and just give me his or her opinion?

Most specialists provide this service. Just make sure you both understand that this is a one-time consultation, and there is no obligation or expectation that you will become an ongoing patient. That means that the consulting doctor will not be responsible for your care after you leave his or her office.

Once you get an accurate diagnosis and a treatment plan, you can ask if the specialist would work with your current local doctor to continue your care or ask the consulting specialist to consider taking you on as a patient.

Should I go to an alternative health practitioner?

There are no alternative treatments that have been demonstrated to be safe and effective for stopping bipolar disorder. However, alternative treatments may be helpful for reducing symptoms of stress, anxiety, and pain. Ask the alternative practitioner to check with your physician to make sure their treatment approach will not interfere with your primary bipolar treatment.

Make sure your alternative practitioner is professional, licensed, and offers to compare the risks and benefits of his or her treatment with mainstream care. If you talk to an alternative care provider who makes promises, acts in an arrogant way, or knocks other professionals, walk out the door. If they charge high fees or want to get you to sign up for treatments in advance, start walking.

It is worth the trouble to find legitimate providers. For example, I know a group of alternative practitioners who are mostly licensed nurses with long patient-care experience. Many of them work out of good hospitals, are professional in speech and demeanor, and are respected by their mainstream colleagues. They are comfortable talking to and working with primary physicians and psychiatrists and will modestly discuss the advantages and disadvantages of their approach. They are caring individuals who will provide references, charge reasonable fees, and will not ask you to commit to treatments in advance. If you want to investigate alternative therapies, look for someone of this caliber.

If you do try an alternative treatment, be sure to keep taking your medications.

Are there fraudulent practitioners out there?

Fraudulent health care is big business. For example, one of my patients told me about her visit to an expensive Beverly Hills doctor for a review of her medications. The doctor asked her to hold her pill bottles in each hand and tell him which felt heavier. From that information, he told her which medications were "best" for her bipolar disorder. I find that pretty scary.

If you find a practitioner who seems fishy, go somewhere else.

5.

PSYCHOTHERAPY

. . . .

For years, reliable research has shown that the best treatment for bipolar disorder is a combination of medications *plus* psychotherapy. In my experience, people who combine psychotherapy with psychopharmacology treatment have about 20 to 50 percent better results than those who try to struggle through with medications alone. If you cannot start them both at the same time, I recommend that medications be started first because good attention, memory, and clear thought processes will be invaluable when you start your psychotherapy.

TYPES OF PSYCHOTHERAPY

There are many types and schools and styles of psychotherapy: cognitive psychotherapy (finding problem thinking patterns), behavioral psychotherapy (learning what to do to feel better), psychodynamic psychotherapy (examining subconscious patterns), interpersonal psychotherapy (examining relationships), reality-based therapy (focusing on the here and now), and family systems therapy (where the family is the focus of inquiry). Educating you about your illness and about how to cope with it is another important focus of psychotherapeutic work for persons with bipolar illness.

What types of psychotherapy are good for bipolar disorder?

I am particularly excited about several psychotherapy techniques that can be adapted to work well in bipolar disorder. Reality-based therapy can be very practical, helping patients in their daily lives, and helping them recognize and change personal and interpersonal habits that they no longer need.

Behavioral therapy can be very helpful in restructuring one's life to include pleasant nonwork activities and to control overfocus on work or social issues. Behavioral therapists are often skilled in teaching stress-reduction techniques.

Interpersonal therapy helps you understand the roles that other people have played in your life. Psychodynamic therapy can help strengthen your boundaries and help you find your own identity. Many other therapeutic approaches can be adapted for treating bipolar disorder. The most important thing is to find a therapist who has a special interest and experience in treating persons with bipolar illness.

What do you do in your psychotherapy with bipolar patients?

I tend to look at interpersonal relationships and interactions. I work together with each patient in analyzing their own interactions, identifying their thoughts and feelings, and understanding how these are communicated. Together we discover how other people think, feel, and interact, and how to interpret the meanings of their interactions and how they affect us. We uncover principles of cause and effect and use them to help reach life goals. This provides a forum for the examination and analysis of all types of life issues as they come up naturally in the course of the therapeutic work.

For bipolar disorder, I think it is important to stay in the present by working on what is happening now. This reduces the stress of painful thoughts and memories and allows patients to gain skills that will help them control their emotions and avoid being controlled by them. I also help patients develop coping strategies and reduce stress by using stress-relieving exercises (see chapter 2).

Q Do I have to dig up old and painful memories?

Your psychotherapy belongs to you. You do not have to do anything that you do not want to do. I think that bipolar psychotherapy should work to keep unpleasant past emotional events under control, rather than to dig them up. Some therapists may not realize that when bipolar patients walk out of the room at the end of their therapy session, they continue to experience painful memories and emotions that may haunt them for hours or days afterward. However, when two people work on present issues and trust develops, old memories often come up on their own at a time when they can be discussed more comfortably and objectively.

For example, I once worked with a bipolar woman who had suffered child abuse from her mother. When we started our psychotherapy, she asked me to promise that I would never try to get her to talk about her mother, to which I agreed. Surprisingly, after we had developed a trusting relationship, she began to mention her mother quite naturally during our discussions. One day she came in and said, "I suddenly realized that I am talking about my mother with you but it doesn't make me upset or depressed." I told her, "I think you are doing fine. Keep 'not talking' about your mother and you will be very happy with the result."

Q I want a therapist to tell me everything is fine, and it will all work out. What's wrong with that?

If therapy is unreasonably optimistic, manics will gain false hope, whereas depressed clients will just be annoyed. The most helpful approach is to encourage complete truth and objectivity in all things.

If I was stranded alone on a deserted island and I had to do my own therapy, what should I do?

You should work to develop objectivity about yourself and the world around you. Check the bibliography at the end of our book for more information on how to do this.

How do I choose between getting psychotherapy or medication treatment?

Who told you that you had to choose? Currently there is an unfortunate turf war between psychopharmacologists and psychotherapists about whether medications or therapy works better. After a lifetime of consideration, I am positive that both are essential to beat bipolar disorder.

Do I need to have a separate therapist and psychiatrist?

You can have whomever you want. If you already have a good therapist when you get your bipolar diagnosis, you probably want to keep them. If not, your psychiatrist may know the names of some good therapists you could consider, or you can look on your own.

Moreover, many psychiatrists offer both medications and psychotherapy. If you have a trusting relationship with your psychiatrist, you may wish to ask them if they would be your therapist as well as your doctor. To minimize confusion on this point, hereafter when I say "doctor" or "therapist" I assume that they might be the same person.

UNDERSTANDING THE DIFFERENCES
BETWEEN TYPES OF THERAPISTS

. . . . . .

- **Psychiatrists** go to school for at least twelve years. They earn a medical doctoral degree (M.D.) and a license to practice general medicine, and complete four years of additional training in psychiatry in an accredited hospital. They learn the biology of emotional illness, the nature of medications and how to use them, and how to perform psychotherapy. Because of this extensive training, psychiatrists often charge higher fees than nonmedical therapists in the same community. Only medical doctors can prescribe medications.
- **Professional Psychologists** earn a Ph.D. degree in a four-year graduate program and usually do a year of practical internship. Many professional psychologists become experts in cognitive and behavioral therapies that can be valuable in the treatment of bipolar disorder. Accredited psychology graduate schools provide very good training, but not all schools are accredited, so it is important to check your psychologist's credentials. Professional psychologists' fees are usually less than physicians' and more than counselors'.
- **Marriage and Family Counselors** complete a two-year graduate degree. They are often trained in family therapy styles. Some, but not all, are interested in bipolar disorder and have experience in its treatment. Family counselors' fees are usually lower than psychiatrists' and professional psychologists' fees.
- **Nurses** attend either a two- or three-year basic nursing program and they may also choose to earn extra certification in mental health nursing. When I worked in a hospital setting, I met many nurses who had great wisdom about psychiatric illness.
- **Social Workers** receive a master's degree in social work (MSW) and are specially trained in the management of moderate and severe mental illness, particularly within the context of public health. They are usually knowledgeable about federal, state, and local services that can help bipolar sufferers and their families. Some social workers provide service at low or deferred fees. Licensed Clinical Social Workers (LCSW) have special training in treating mental illness. I know several social workers who have chosen to become familiar with the special problems of bipolar disorder.

Q My acting coach acts like a therapist, but I'm feeling worse and worse. Why is this?

From the beginning of method acting, there has been a connection between Freudian psychology and schools of drama and acting. Unfortunately, when some acting teachers try to take on the role of therapists, they do more harm than good. Usually the problem is that bipolar students are forced to reexperience all kinds of emotional traumas. Once started, these painful thoughts and emotions keep coming back again and again.

THE BENEFITS OF PSYCHOTHERAPY FOR BIPOLAR DISORDER

Psychotherapy is more than just talking with your friends. It is a detailed, interactive process that takes years to learn and decades of experience to perfect. Good psychotherapy is quite difficult to explain, but it can be experienced as improved functioning in your life.

Q What good will psychotherapy do for my bipolar disorder?

Bipolar disorder is a stress-related illness. By reducing stress, psychotherapy can reduce the physiological problems of bipolar disorder. Psychotherapy can also help you reverse harmful patterns of behavior that you have acquired as a result of having bipolar disorder. It has been shown that patients tolerate side effects and take medications more regularly and more correctly when they are in regular therapeutic contact with a clinician. Regular clinical sessions can help you become sensitive to the actions of the illness in your life and help you anticipate impending manic or depressive swings. Psychotherapy can help you better understand the nature of bipolar illness and develop the coping skills necessary to deal with it.

What else can psychotherapy help me with?

Psychotherapy can help you formulate and fulfill your life goals, deal with your interpersonal issues, gain insight into your actions and those of others, and develop improved strategies of living your life more efficiently, effectively, and successfully.

WHY BIPOLAR DISORDER CANNOT BE TREATED WITH PSYCHOTHERAPY ALONE

. . . . . .

In bipolar disorder, there is a part of the brain that is not functioning the way it should. Medicine is the only thing we have to make the brain function like it was designed to function. Bipolar disorder produces problems in mental functions like attention/distractibility, memory, and multistep reasoning. Without medications, impaired thinking makes it difficult to make progress in life and in psychotherapy. Some court cases have even argued that it is malpractice to treat bipolar disorder with psychotherapy alone. Psychotherapy cannot prevent the onset of depression, mania, or psychosis. Medications are all we have now to keep bipolar episodes from recurring and making the disease worse.

Your best chance to have a great life is to stabilize your bipolar disorder with mood stabilizers, learn everything you can about bipolar disorder, and manage your stress with psychotherapy. If it helps, think of it like this: Would you rather take medications and make three years' progress in one year, or avoid medications and make one year's progress in three years?

CHOOSING A THERAPIST

Because there is such a confusing array of types of therapists and styles of therapy, the task of choosing a therapist can be daunting. Here are some suggestions to get you started.

I just found out I have bipolar disorder, but I already have a therapist. Should I get a new one?

Not necessarily. If you already have a good working relationship with a therapist, then you should consider staying with that person. You will need a professional you can trust to help you battle bipolar illness. If your current therapist does not know a lot about bipolar disorder, you might like to start by looking through this book together.

How do I know if a therapist is qualified enough for me?

The most important qualification for a therapist is whether or not they are good at what they do. For example, there are plenty of mature therapists who are terrific at what they do, even if they do not follow the latest fads in psychotherapy. There are also plenty of younger therapists who are wise beyond their years. When you find a gem of a therapist, hang on to them.

What's the best way to find a new therapist?

The best sources of information are the recommendations from doctors that you trust and from friends and family who like their therapists and have been making lots of progress in their psychotherapy. You can sometimes hear therapists speak at university seminars and bipolar association meetings. Check chapter 10 for contact information. You can also attend local meetings and bipolar support groups to listen to other patients talk about what they like and do not like about their own therapists.

What should I consider when checking out potential therapists?

Try to find a therapist who has had experience with bipolar patients in the past and is willing to understand your illness. If therapists are licensed in your state, contact your state board of physicians, psychologists, counselors, social workers, etc. to make sure that your potential therapist is licensed in good standing. Anyone with bipolar disorder should make it a priority to see clinicians who are licensed by their state and/or a national credentialing board. You can also make sure that your prospective therapists have never lost their licenses or been suspended for professional malpractice or misconduct.

Therapists' credentials include the number of years they have practiced or, if the therapist is young, the program where they trained. For therapists who do not have a private practice, the institutions where they work now and where they have worked in the past can sometimes be illuminating. Publications such as research papers or a regular column in a professional journal are good, but they do not necessarily prove that anyone is a good therapist. If therapists have written a book, look to see if it is a legitimate, professional publication from a major publisher. Do not be influenced by a fancy office, awards, or diplomas on the wall.

Is there anything I can do before I make an appointment?

Yes. Call up and talk with your prospective therapist about where they went to school, how long they have been in practice, how many bipolar clients they have worked with during their career, and how many bipolar patients they have now. Ask them how their treatment for persons with bipolar disorder differs from what they provide for their other clients.

Who's cheapest to see, a psychiatrist, a psychologist, a counselor, a social worker, or my family doctor?

You will hear all sorts of answers to this question, hinging on issues of insurance, fees, seeing one person instead of two, and so forth. The answer is simply that the least expensive form of treatment is the one that keeps you most healthy. The big costs of bipolar disorder are in dollars and broken dreams that come from disease episodes, not from doctors' and therapists' fees.

Why is it that when I look in the telephone book most therapists never mention what kind of therapy they do?

I have wondered about this for years. In order to find out the type of therapy they do you must contact the therapist and ask them directly. Consider asking, "What kind of therapy were you trained in?" or "What therapy model do you use?" You should be concerned if a therapist cannot tell you clearly what type of psychotherapy they are trained in.

How can I stop my brother from spending all his time in therapy trying to convince his therapist that he does not have bipolar disorder?

Bipolar individuals who waste their therapy appointments arguing that they are really fine are only exposing their fear of illness and sabotaging the work that could be making their life better. Sometimes patients in denial must stop psychotherapy until they can admit that they have a problem and commit themselves to working on it until they are healthy.

What can I do to supplement my psychotherapy?

Join national bipolar disorder associations, read newsletters and magazines published by professionals about bipolar disorder, and look into support groups available locally or online. The resources in chapter 10 will give you some information to get you started.

THE FOUR STAGES OF BIPOLAR RECOVERY

* * * * * *

Attitude is important, and I am often asked what kind of attitude is necessary in order to beat bipolar disorder. I have divided the recovery process into four stages, along with affirmations for you to make that will help you progress to full health and maintain it.

Stage I: Accepting that there is something wrong with you that requires treatment.
Affirmation: "I am not perfect."

Stage II: Accepting that you must take medication and make sacrifices every day to maintain your health.
Affirmation: "I do not always know what is best for me.
I must follow rules that I did not make up."

Stage III: Accepting that you truly have a disease called bipolar disorder that will never go away.
Affirmation: "My life will not be flawless,
but I will work to ensure that my life is good."

Stage IV: Making a lifetime commitment to learn all you can about bipolar disorder and taking responsibility for the details of your health at all times.
Affirmation: "I cannot rely on fate. I will take responsibility
for myself and create my own destiny."

6.

PRACTICAL LIFE
STRATEGIES FOR
CAREER SUCCESS

. . . .

We must all learn to use our skills and talents to their fullest. In order to handle day-to-day challenges in work and career, we depend on both our common sense and what we have learned from handling the same situations in the past. However, bipolar disorder can make it difficult to respond naturally and can interfere with the ability to learn from past experience. To compensate for this, I encourage my patients to develop special strategies to handle a variety of situations that are especially challenging for those with bipolar illness.

UNDERSTANDING YOUR STRENGTHS
AND WEAKNESSES

Many people with bipolar disorder are particularly good at creative tasks that require brainstorming, conceptualizing, and finding new ideas. These special talents get stronger with treatment. Creative jobs are found in music, art, writing, acting, design, and many other areas.

How can I best use my creativity in my career?

You can get the best use from your creativity by getting it under control. You want to be able to create what you want when you want to create it without having to wait for inspiration to strike. For example, if you are a writer you cannot sit around waiting for the muse to inspire you before beginning. Instead, you must be able to work on your craft every day. However, before you can get your creativity under control, you first must have your bipolar disorder under control.

What is it about detailed tasks that makes them so hard for me?

Bipolar disorder seems to make it harder to handle details or to juggle several separate tasks at the same time without becoming overwhelmed. Attending to details often requires that you maintain several steps in your mind at the same time. Tasks involving minor details and steplike logic may be harder for persons with bipolar disorder than other tasks that appear to be less difficult. For example, I have known bipolar patients who were brilliant university professors but could not balance their checkbooks every month. They had found careers that emphasized their strengths.

I get one step away from having everything I want and then I blow it. Am I afraid to succeed?

Everyone is afraid of success somewhere inside themselves, just as everyone has some fear of the unknown. Fear of embarrassment or humiliation can stifle progress in a career.

For example, Oscar Levant was a wonderful musician and performer who often played piano at the parties of his many celebrity friends. Later in life, when he was down and out, his friends invited big-name producers and directors to their parties to meet him. All he would have had to do was show off his musical genius at the piano and he would have been offered high-paying jobs that he desperately needed. Unfortunately, when the host had gathered the VIPs around the piano, Mr. Levant would look up at them, grin, and begin to play "Mary Had a Little Lamb."

I do not think this is fear of success. It is more like fear of being judged less than wonderful and suffering internal humiliation. Do not waste brain space worrying about success or failure and you will have more resources to devote to your success.

Why do I always put things off until the last minute?

You may realize that at the last moment, under the threat of failure, you can force yourself to finish everything in one marathon session. This approach often works, but it does not produce your best work. Procrastination and difficulty finishing projects are major sources of problems for people with bipolar disorder. Mania predisposes individuals to start interesting new projects that often drag on and become too complicated to complete. Bipolar depression makes it difficult to start any projects at all.

Typically, it is difficult to start projects during a period of bipolar depression and difficult to finish projects in periods of both bipolar depression and mania. This could be a neurophysiological part of bipolar disease that involves brain centers that control initiating and stopping physical actions (see chapter 1).

I procrastinate and I can't seem to finish my projects on time. Is this part of bipolar disorder?

Yes. Bipolar disorder can make it difficult to initiate and finish tasks. This often shows up as procrastination, and doing all your work at the last minute is not a prescription for success.

For example, I once worked with a successful author who procrastinated. She told me how she had once kept a rental video for a year. Although she passed the video rental store every day, she was not able to return it. Fortunately, we worked hard on procrastination in her therapy that year and she was able to write and submit two excellent novels on time. This was a first in her career.

DEFINING CAREER SUCCESS

Some of the biggest career challenges experienced by individuals with bipolar disorder include finding the right career, avoiding overwork, and maintaining appropriate interactions with supervisors and coworkers. If you prepare yourself to address workplace issues in advance, you have the best chance of a wonderful career experience.

Are there any careers that people with bipolar disorder can't do?

Whereas you may have to work harder to accomplish your goals because you have bipolar disorder, I have no doubt that you can do anything you want with your life. The challenge is to make sure that you choose a life-style that you will really enjoy.

How can I be a success?

You must decide what you mean when you say success. Suppose your idea of success is making money. Then do some research in the library or on the Internet and find a list of the careers that have higher incomes. You can choose among the ones that appeal to you.

On the other hand, suppose that your idea of success is to be married and have a family. Then you want to be looking for a job that has good benefits, is close to home, and will allow you enough time to enjoy your family life. Some businesses are particularly pro-family, and you might want to look for these.

Some people value spirituality in their lives. They may have a nasty shock if they wake up one day and realize that their career and their need for spiritual fulfillment are competing with each other. If they had defined their personal idea of success, they would have begun by choosing a job that would support their own spiritual values.

Whatever you want out of life, you must first define what success means to you before you can be successful. It all depends on you.

SEVEN QUESTIONS TO ASK YOURSELF
WHEN CHOOSING A CAREER

. . . .

1. Do you like to spend the day sitting, standing, talking, working with your hands, or interacting with people face-to-face?
2. In what type of location do you prefer to work?
3. What types of people do you feel comfortable around?
4. Do you prefer to interact with lots of supportive coworkers, or do you prefer to be left alone to do your work?
5. Do you feel more comfortable when someone is helping you avoid mistakes, or do you resent supervision and "micromanagement"?
6. Do you like to work at a desk?
7. Do you like to talk over the telephone?

It is important that you not only like your job intellectually, but that you also are able to fill your days with people and tasks that you enjoy. These are the things that will determine how well you will like a job day by day and moment by moment.

What are the simplest things I can do to maximize my chances for career success?

I can reduce the majority of career challenges to four factors: keep yourself healthy, minimize stress, keep out of interpersonal problems, and try to be yourself.

Are there any jobs I should avoid?

I think that you can probably do well at almost any job. However, you may feel better in a low-stress career. Your bipolar disorder is a stress-related illness—the more stress you experience; the harder it will be to stay healthy. Your first priority should be looking after your health. Demanding careers, like being a stockbroker, often require you to focus all of your energy on your job and would make it difficult for you to stay healthy.

I encourage my patients to find work that is low-key, low-stress, relaxing, and pleasant. I advise looking for a work environment that is comfortable without being boring. Try to find a situation where coworkers are tolerant and mutually supportive. Look for short hours, a regular daytime schedule, no night work, friendly people, and a nonhierarchical, cooperative work style (that is, where you have freedom to work independently without overbearing supervision). Many people with bipolar disorder have found success starting their own businesses, especially when they start small with low stress and build them up over time.

This is my fourth job in a year, and I'm sick of it already. How can I find a job that I enjoy?

Let's face it: all work is somewhat unpleasant or else people would do it for free. After all, that is why they call it work. In bipolar disorder, there is also a strong tendency to criticize oneself needlessly for not having done something better. Do not be hard on yourself. "What might have been" is only a fantasy, and fantasies do not put bread on the table. If you have a career that works fairly well, keep it and try to improve the experience of it.

What do I do if I can't be a success in my career?

Career success is not everything. If you spend all your time and energy on your career, when will you be able to sit back and enjoy life? If you get a simple, stable job that pays enough money plus good benefits and allows you plenty of extra time to do what you really want, you could have the means to do something creative, to travel, have a family, volunteer, or just relax and enjoy life. There are many prescriptions for success.

INTERVIEWING AND GETTING A JOB

You will probably have to pass an interview to get the job you want. By honing your interviewing skills, you can make people want to help you out in your chosen career.

How can I best showcase my talents without bragging?

Do not keep quiet about your specialness out of misplaced modesty. Mention your talents when they come up in the conversation but do not dwell on them.

How should I conduct myself during a job interview?

Wear conservative clothing, write a clear résumé, be yourself, and do not argue with the interviewer. You cannot imagine how many people with bipolar disorder have lost jobs because they became embroiled in a disagreement during their job interview.

Understand that an interview is a special exercise to get a job, and it is not just two people talking together in a room. You have to be a negotiator and turn questions to your advantage. You must also remember to keep your responses positive. I know a talented man who had found a great job he desperately wanted. Everything was going well until the interviewer asked him what he found wrong with the job. He replied, "Oh, it's too hot, it's not a nice neighborhood, I would prefer to work with younger people, etc." At that point, the interviewer stopped the interview and sent him home. If he had just said, "I think I could be very happy working here," he would have been given the job.

How can I write a good résumé and use it to get a job?

Many people with bipolar disorder have trouble being succinct. For your résumé, put all your information on one page with one-inch margins and 14-point type. This will force you to eliminate the excess verbiage. Then, take copies with you to your interview so you and your interviewer can look at your résumé during your meeting. It is much easier for you to have a pleasant discussion about what is on your résumé than to try to field a bunch of unpredictable questions.

What if I make a mistake and say the wrong thing during the interview?

During the stress of an interview, bipolar sufferers run the risk of speaking impulsively. The easiest thing to do is to say something like, "You know, I was thinking more about the question you asked me and I'd like to revise my answer. What I really wanted to say was . . ." Do not think that everything you say has to be perfect.

DECREASE YOUR STRESS AT THE WORKPLACE

Bipolar disorder is a stress-related illness, and stress will make it worse. It is well worth your while to track down sources of stress and avoid or eliminate them in order to become more happy and efficient at work.

Why can some people stop after working eight hours, but I feel like I have to work all the time?

Your problem could be that you are not using efficient time-management skills. Many bipolar people tend to work slowly or spend too much time on details that are not essential to the task. Are you trying to do a better job than you are being asked to do? Are you daydreaming or otherwise wasting time? Manic experience tends to make individuals with bipolar illness try to work too long and too hard, but you need to relax if you want to stay healthy.

Is it healthy that I have to work so late that I only have time to work, eat, and go to bed?

Because bipolar individuals often experience a burst of energy in the evening, they tend to put in long evening hours. You cannot have bipolar disorder and be healthy if you overwork yourself. Working yourself to the bone causes burnout, and depression is sure to follow. Take stock of your situation and make sure your workload is not compromising your health.

How can I keep my boss from asking me to do
    extra work? I always end up working
    too late.

Say "No." It seems too simple but that is the solution. Try playacting the situation with your friends, family, and/or therapist. Look online to see how other people with bipolar disorder handled this problem in their lives (see chapter 10, Resources). Practice saying "No" comfortably, convincingly, and unemotionally. If this does not work, talk with your human resources representative to ensure that your schedule is appropriate and healthy for you.

My boss is always looking at my behind and
    commenting on it, but he says it's only a
    natural reaction to my good looks. It still
    makes me uncomfortable. What can I do?

Engaging sociability and personal magnetism accentuated by bipolar disorder often make bipolar individuals the targets of inappropriate behavior. I advise you to take a trip down to the human resources office and tell them what's going on. If they are not outraged or look like they are siding with your boss, take the matter up with your attorney. Do not tolerate sexism on the job.

Why is it that when I really seem to be
    making progress in my career, my
    bipolar illness gets worse and things
    get screwed up?

Maybe you are working and concentrating on your career so hard that you let your overall health slide. Are you sleeping reasonable hours? Is your nutrition good? Are you getting exercise? Are you getting regular rest and relaxation? It is not much use working hard if you neglect your health and get struck down by your bipolar disorder.

DEALING WITH SUPERVISORS AND COWORKERS

Career success is usually correlated with your effectiveness at dealing with other people. Honing your skills at work relationships and avoiding social pitfalls will help you work more effectively and more successfully.

Q **Why do I find everyone at work so intimidating? I'm afraid they'll find out I'm not qualified.**

This is a common fear in persons with bipolar disorder, usually stemming from a combination of self-doubt and depression. If you have been doing your work well, that is usually enough. Do not be so hard on yourself.

Q **Will my supervisor really mind if I come in late or miss a day since I put in extra hours?**

Because of their reversed sleep-wake cycle, bipolar employees often find it hard to get up in the morning and easy to overwork at night. Bear in mind that employees are usually criticized if they are not at their jobs, whether they have been working extra hours or not. Try to stick to the regular schedule, and you will be happier.

Q **I try to be a good employee by doing extra work but they are never satisfied. Why?**

Be careful if you are trying to work extra hard to get the approval of your supervisors and employers. Sometimes the desire to impress by overworking backfires. For example, it is easy for supervisors and coworkers to assume that this is your baseline and expect you to do more all the time. If you can be yourself and do a reasonable job, you can be a good employee and stay healthy, too.

Why can't I stand up to my boss when I want something?

It is best that you do not "stand up" to anyone out of impatience or anger. Wait until you are not angry and try to find a more congenial way to get what you want. For example, find a time when things are going well to suggest to your boss calmly that you would like a raise. You can practice the situation beforehand with your friends, family, and/or your therapist. Role-play an interaction, like asking for a raise in salary, from both sides until you understand what both people are feeling. Then you will be more comfortable asking for what you need.

Why is it that I do a better job than all my workmates, but they get promoted and I don't?

The most frequent reasons that bipolar persons I know do not get promoted include working too late, working too much, talking to or trying to help others too much, and failure to fit into the work group. It is not enough just to do a better job than others. Ask your boss what you specifically need to do to advance to a higher level. My suggestion is to minimize your ego connection with your job and to focus on being a better, equal team player.

BOUNDARY ISSUES IN THE WORKPLACE

Social boundaries refer to the imaginary wall that separates us from others. In bipolar disorder, this wall is often "leaky," so that parts of other people's experience can leak in and feel like they are part of you. The ability to separate yourself from others in your mind is part of what will allow you to have a strong and healthy sense of self-identity.

I constantly worry about what everybody else at the office thinks of me. Can I learn to stop?

When boundaries are leaky, it can seem that other people's feelings toward you determine who you really are. Perhaps you feel that others' personalities have partially merged with yours. For example, if you are imagining that you know what somebody is thinking about you, stop and check your own boundaries. You will realize that what you imagine is in other people's minds is a fantasy within you and not part of the real world. You are a self-sufficient person who is not dependent on other people's opinions.

However, if you find that the opinions of others obsessively dominate your mind and you cannot get them out of your thoughts, you may be facing a biochemical problem. See your doctor and make sure that you are taking mood stabilizers and/or other medications that stop intrusive and circular thoughts.

Why shouldn't I run around and get everyone's opinion before I make a decision?

Boundary issues combined with heightened concern with what others think complicate decision-making in bipolar disorder. It may seem that you must combine everyone's opinions together with yours. However, you do not want to be dependent on others to make your decisions for you. Moreover, you may put others off if you ask their advice and then do not take it. If you focus hard enough, I expect that you can make better decisions on your own, and it is good practice to do so. If you need feedback, find the best person to ask, but do not spend your time shopping around for opinions.

I try to be helpful to everyone all the time, but they don't offer to help me. Why?

Weak social boundaries can make it feel like other people's work and responsibilities belong to you. However, it is not your job to do other people's work for them. Just concentrate on doing your own job well. When you offer to help people at work, it may remind them that they cannot do the task by themselves or that you think they cannot do their job well. They may even end up resenting you for your efforts to help. Instead, try helping others by offering encouragement and a positive outlook and see how things go.

Why do I have a feeling that I am personally responsible for the success of the company?

This is the most frequent career problem that I hear about from my bipolar patients. Leaky boundaries can cause you to feel that you and your workmates are intertwined and you are responsible for everyone.

You probably are a cog in the machine rather than the hub. Unless you are the head of the company, you are not responsible for its welfare. Your health, not the company, is your first responsibility. Go ahead and do a good day's work. Then forget about it, go home, and relax.

How can I tell my coworkers and supervisors that they are doing things all wrong?

When boundaries blur, it may seem perfectly reasonable to tell other people how to do their work, just as you tell yourself how to do your work. However, people are entitled to make their own mistakes and you are not responsible. Try to focus on your own work and let everyone else do theirs in their own way. Do not fantasize about how you could be running the company better.

Should I tell people at work that I'm bipolar? For some reason, I think they know it already.

With leaky social boundaries, it can seem that everyone knows everything about you that you know yourself. However, I do not advise patients to tell others in the workplace about their illness. For one thing, many of the feelings in bipolar disorder have to be experienced to be understood. Moreover, bipolar disorder is a complicated disease and most people know little about it. This could create tension between you and your coworkers due to misconceptions and stigma regarding the illness.

Everyone at work is so nice. I want them all to be a part of my life.

When social boundaries are weak in bipolar disorder, it can seem like other people share your same sense of fairness, loyalty, consideration, and empathy, but you may be surprised. Workplace relationships may involve competition, self-interest, and disregard for your feelings. For example, if you give a coworker personal information and it is spread all over the office, it could be embarrassing and a hindrance to your ability to work comfortably in your career.

Why shouldn't I want everyone at work to be my personal friend?

It's very important to be congenial and positive when at work, join in when groups go out to lunch, and so forth. However, business relationships are very different from personal friendships, and mixing the two often causes problems. If you want to have a coworker as a friend, it is better to treat them as a workmate during work and save the friendship part for after working hours.

I've dated and become intimate with several coworkers in the office. What's wrong with that?

Many people have social and sexual fantasies about their workmates. However, weakened boundaries, heightened sociability, and hypersexuality caused by bipolar disorder can lead you to seek too much intimacy with those around you. Do the people you have dated in the office respect you as a coworker and a professional, or do they see you as a sexual partner? You must retain workmates' respect to be effective in your career.

WORK ATTITUDES AND VULNERABILITIES

As you know, attitude is very important. When you have bipolar disorder, you are more vulnerable to irritability, distractibility, and interpersonal problems. In the workplace, these vulnerabilities can keep you from doing your job well and they can make a bad impression on your bosses. In particular, try to leave your personal emotions and ego at home, so you can do your job smoothly and efficiently.

I don't care about deadlines. I want my project to be perfect.

Just make sure the people you work for feel the same way. Oftentimes supervisors and coworkers care more about their deadlines than perfection. Remember that your missed deadline may affect other people and their ability to do their jobs.

I try to bend over backward to be tolerant to annoying and unfair people, but eventually I blow up.

Try not to be so tolerant. When minor issues come up, address them positively and constructively. It is always easier to wait until you blow up with anger, but that will not help you make progress in your career.

Why do people think I'm angry? I *am* angry but I never show it.

I once worked with a bipolar woman who was very angry inside but prided herself on never, ever showing it at work. One day she caught a look at her personnel file and found it was full of comments about how angry she was. Other people can notice anger even if you try not to show it.

How can I deal with my anger in a positive way?

Start by realizing that the emotion of anger is not bad; only the expression of that anger in words, thoughts, and actions is bad. Learn to follow your level of stress and frustration so that you are prepared to head off anger before it bursts into your words and thoughts. Prepare yourself before going into situations where your anger is likely to be provoked. Come up with options to releasing anger in specific stressful situations and practice them. Role-play irritating situations with friends and family until you can understand how each person in a disagreement feels. Discuss your anger issues with a support group or in an online forum (see chapter 10, Resources). If your anger comes out most when you feel threatened or ashamed, ask your therapist to work on issues of vulnerability and self-doubt.

Can medication help with my irritability problem? I always end up arguing with the boss and getting in trouble.

It is okay to be irritable, but if you cannot keep your emotions and comments under control, then you need to address this in your treatment. Often the problem is that emotions like anger come out so rapidly that you do not have any chance to stop them.

Medications can help in two ways. They can help lower your overall anger level, and can also help you keep anger from coming out so quickly and impulsively. I try to use mood stabilizers like carbamazepine, lithium salt, or clonidine because they can reduce anger while they treat underlying bipolar disorder.

Q Why does my boss think I'm just "futzing around" when I'm trying to prevent future problems? I call it failure planning.

Usually it is more efficient to handle problems after they begin to appear. It can become a full-time job if you try to anticipate every possible future problem and solve it in advance.

Q How can I keep from being distracted at work by calls and interruptions? It completely sets me back.

Distractibility caused by bipolar disorder can make you particularly vulnerable to calls and interruptions. You have to remove the immediacy from these contacts. Let your calls go to a message machine that you check on a schedule. Try not to let your coworkers and employees interrupt you. Instead, decide on regular times when you will be available and get people used to contacting you at those times.

Q I'm addicted to solitaire, and now I play it all day, even at work. I'm afraid I'm going to get fired. What can I do to stop?

Computer and Internet addictions represent real dangers to everyone, especially persons with bipolar disorder who are easily distracted. Take drastic actions. Erase the addresses of Internet sites where you waste time from your bookmarks and favorite site listings on your computer. Erase game programs on your computer. Set up "Internet-free" periods and stick to them. I knew a brilliant man who finally cut the cord of his mouse and learned all the keyboard commands to do his work. Without the mouse, he could not play games, and without the ability to play games, he broke his gaming habit.

Could e-mail be reducing my productivity at work?

Distractible individuals run the risk of spending all of their time checking, reading, and replying to e-mail. Set aside specific times to check your e-mail, which allow you sufficient time to work without distraction.

Why does my boss think I am too intense?

People who are bipolar often come across as too strong and too persistent. While there is nothing wrong with being intense, you do not want to seem intrusive. You can use your coworkers' behavior as a guide to the level of interaction appropriate to your work situation.

Why do my coworkers say I am inconsiderate of other people's feelings when I think I tell things the way they are?

Before you speak, try to envision what effect your actions will have on others. Be conscious of your intention in each communication: for example, are you serious, jesting, reassuring, or asking for help? Keep mental notes on how people react to your tone, speech style, attempts at humor, and so forth so you can be sure you do not make other people feel bad.

Why should I be punished because I can't get along with impossible people? I think they are the ones who should be punished.

Yes, it does not seem fair. However, at some time everyone has to deal with difficult people. Fair or not, if you are not able to get along with an annoying supervisor or exasperating coworker, then you will not be viewed as a team player, and it is you who will end up being punished.

Why should I only get one week of vacation when my boss gets three, and he can't do anything right?

It is universal for persons with bipolar disorder to compare themselves with others. However, things are not always equitable. The most important approach is to avoid fantasizing about how the world *might* have been, and exercise humility and respect for others. If you become the boss, someday you may have three weeks of vacation, too.

I get upset when I'm told to do things by people who are stupid and don't do their job as well as I do.

You can get upset at injustices or at the incompetence of others, or you can choose not to, but you need to understand that these situations are common to most workplaces. Your supervisors do not want to know that you could run things better than they can. Supervisors are looking out for their own careers, not yours. If you want to run things then you should become the supervisor. Until then, don't shoot yourself in the foot by alienating the people you work for.

Why should I have to do my job if all of the other employees aren't doing theirs?

You will have to do your job if you want to get paid. Unfortunately, the world is not fair and you have to play by the rules, regardless of what other people do. Most people know this already, so if you are considering leaving your job because you see others who are not doing theirs, you may be on the brink of a manic episode. Focus on being logical and make sure you are not slipping into poor mental health. If you have any doubts, take it up with your doctor.

DISABILITY

Some people cannot sustain the stress of working without getting sick from their bipolar disorder. Be assured that these individuals are not lazy people; they want to do their part like everyone else. Even though they cannot work at a job, they volunteer, do public service, and help care for others during the day.

What is "disability status"?

Disability status entitles you to income, medical care, and social support through national social security or state disability programs. Disability status can be temporary, where you are expected to go back to work in a matter of months, or permanent, where it is assumed you will not be able to return to the workforce for several years or perhaps not at all.

FIVE MAJOR CAUSES OF DISABILITY IN BIPOLAR DISORDERS

1. The inability to keep a regular work schedule
2. The inability to work under stress
3. The inability to get along with supervisors and coworkers
4. The inability to complete complex tasks on time
5. Delusions of persecution on the job

Should I take a month off work in order to get healthy?

On the surface, this sounds like a great idea, but I've never seen it work out in bipolar disorder. Usually people with bipolar disorder have a number of activities planned during the time they are supposed to be recuperating. They are seldom ready to go back to work after a month, and I have seen many of these "month-off" disabilities end up worsening bipolar symptoms and turning into permanent unemployment. Instead, make sure you are not doing extra work that is not essential, use your free time to do more enjoyable, relaxing things, and make sure your sleep and eating habits are healthy. If that is not enough, see if you can work one hour less each day. If your work still interferes with your health too much, then reconsider your choice of job: it may not be right for you.

I feel guilty about taking long-term disability. Isn't it like taking charity?

Actually, you are entitled to the money if your illness is so bad that you cannot work. If you have worked before, then you have already paid into the disability fund yourself.

A SEVEN-STEP PLAN FOR SUCCESS IN THE WORKPLACE

. . . .

1. Figure out what you mean by success and then seek it.
2. Make your health your first priority.
3. Find a career where the surroundings are comfortable and the details of your daily work activities are pleasant.
4. Do not base your self-esteem on outside achievements. Work for peace, satisfaction, and inner fulfillment.
5. Do not try to be a hero. Just do a reasonable job in a reasonable time.
6. Use your doctor and therapist to help you cope.
7. If you cannot succeed at what you are trying to do, be flexible enough to change directions.

7.

FINDING AND MAINTAINING HEALTHY PERSONAL RELATIONSHIPS

. . . .

Social contact and successful personal relationships are important parts of normal living. Many people with bipolar disorder are lonely and cannot seem to find or hang on to the life partners they want and need. This may result from communication difficulties, the ups and downs of mood swings, or even the intensity of interactions in bipolar disorder. Finding relationship strategies that work for you can help you develop the personal life that you want and deserve.

MAKING CONVERSATION

Starting and keeping personal relationships requires good communication. You will want to know what to say and when to say it, especially when getting to know potential partners.

What do I do if there's a silence during a conversation?

If a quiet moment ensues, then so be it. It is a natural part of healthy communication. It is not your responsibility to keep everyone entertained. In fact, people would rather direct their own conversation than have you do it for them. Let people do what's natural for them and enjoy whatever comes up.

People always try to break away when I'm
    talking to them. What am I doing wrong?

Are you talking too much without letting anyone get a word in edgewise?
Keep the conversation time equal. After you have made a point, wait until
the other person speaks and finishes what they are saying before you start
talking again.

Lately my partner has stopped talking to me.
    Should I look for someone else?

Show your partner that you are interested in what he or she has to say. Respond by listening with an appropriate expression on your face and do not
interrupt or insert your own observations. This may help start up the conversation again.

Everyone says I'm a great conversationalist.
    Can I use that to dazzle my dates?

Sure, you could if you wanted to. However, I think that most good relationship partners would rather spend quiet time with someone who is gen-
uine than be dazzled all evening. The circus is a dazzling experience, but
people do not want to go there every day.

I always say whatever comes into my head, and
    sometimes it isn't very nice. Can I fix this?

This is pretty common, particularly in mania, where it is caused by bipolar
disorder. Address physiological problems by strengthening your medications. Practice previewing everything you say in your mind before you say
it. In your spare time, practice counting to two before you make any state-
ment. Continually remind yourself of your surroundings and make sure
your content and style of communication are appropriate and inoffensive.

LEARN TO MAKE SMALL TALK:
A THREE-STEP METHOD
· · · · · ·

Bipolar disorder often brings the gift of gab but some people tell me that they have trouble making small talk. They are happy to find out that making small talk is a skill that can be learned easily. I have formulated a simple method. After mastering this strategy for small talk, one of my patients told me, "Now I'm a social butterfly."

1. Make sure that you demonstrate that you are a good listener.
2. Ask the other person open-ended questions about themselves to start and maintain your conversation.
3. In general, try to avoid talking about yourself, at least at first.

In order to make people want to talk to you, you must show that you are interested in hearing what they have to say. Look at their lips when they are speaking and do not be afraid to smile. Make sure that you nod your head and say things like "yes," "uh-huh," and "I see" periodically so they know you are following what they are saying. If you want a general rule, try to make some comment after every five sentences that the other person speaks.

Ask leading, open-ended questions like, "Well what did you think about . . ." or, "How did you get interested in . . . ?" or, "I've always wanted to learn more about . . ." Asking open-ended questions will help you avoid any kind of reply that can be completed with a "yes" or "no," or another question. People love to talk about themselves and when they do, it takes away your responsibility to come up with conversation topics.

In general, try to avoid talking about yourself, at least at first. You may not be comfortable talking about yourself with strangers, and some aggressive conversationalists can make it seem like you are being cross-examined. If the conversation gets too personal, just say, "Let's talk about something else."

If you find something about yourself that you do want to talk about, watch the person with whom you are speaking to make sure you do not talk more about yourself than they talk about themselves.

Learn these principles and role-play conversations alone and with friends, family members, and/or your therapist. Go to support groups and online forums and do not be afraid to speak up (see chapter 10, Resources). Then take every opportunity to practice in real group settings until you are happy with your schmoozing ability.

SOCIALIZING

Bipolar disorder affects the ability to socialize. Generally, increased sociability goes with mania and social avoidance goes with bipolar depression, but often the two are mixed.

Q **People tell me I'm intense, but I don't want to be. What can I do to keep from seeming intense?**

You cannot help being who you are. However, if you want to avoid looking intense, try to slow down and relax whenever you are around other people. That will help them relax, and they will want to interact with you more instead of feeling pressured.

Q **Why can't I predict what my friends will do next? Everyone's responses seem pretty random to me.**

Growing up with bipolar disorder may have long-term effects on how you perceive others' actions. Young children with bipolar disorder often have cognitive problems (including poor concentration and difficulty understanding cause and effect). This can make adults' behavior seem unpredictable, random, and purposeless.

As an adult, check yourself to be sure you are in the habit of remembering each individual's past behavior as a way of predicting their actions in the future. Try to get a sense of people's personalities, so you can say, "This person is like this, so she will usually do that." There is usually a cause and effect relationship in all human behavior. Try to understand how others are thinking differently than you. Ask your family and friends to explain why they do and think the things they do. Discuss the issue in support groups or in online forums (see chapter 10, Resources). Ask your therapist to work on interpersonal interactions in your psychotherapy until you can better predict how others will respond to you.

Q I do not have any problem socializing. Everyone loves me, and they want to be around me all the time. Everyone thinks I'm perfect and wonderful, and I think so, too.

I often hear this said, but I have never seen anyone, bipolar or not, whose friends and workmates think that they are completely perfect and wonderful. Manic experience gives rise to feelings that we are more popular and more wonderful than we really are (often called grandiosity). Try talking to other people about your faults and how they think you can improve your social behavior. If you are falling into a manic episode, see your doctor and strengthen your medications before your life gets out of control.

LOVE RELATIONSHIPS

Sometimes growing up bipolar makes it difficult to learn about deep love in interpersonal relationships. True love comes from a connection with another that does not depend on any intellectual analysis. It is almost visceral—a tightness or hurt inside you. It is what makes you want to be with another person, and it has nothing to do with how they look or act.

Q I didn't get along with my parents so I don't have a role model for love. Is it like how I feel about babies and puppies?

If you have a deep and healthy connection with a parent, grandparent, aunt, or uncle, then you can get an idea of what love is like from how you feel about them. Unfortunately, it is sometimes hard to understand the love experience if your parent(s) are bipolar and cannot provide a healthy model. Most people agree that love feels like a warm, caring connection that emanates from the chest, separate from intellectual thoughts. If you have never felt love for an adult before, the love you feel for babies and puppies may point you in the right direction.

I suddenly realized I'm in love with someone other than my spouse. Should I ask for a divorce?

Emotions can change quickly in bipolar disorder. Make sure your illness is under control and then wait before making any rash decisions. Step away from the relationship temporarily and see if you still feel the same way after a month or two. Remember that secret liaisons can seem especially attractive because of their secrecy, and they may not be based on actual love.

The emotions of bipolar individuals can easily go to extremes. It may become easy to fall in love with someone that has no potential for a healthy relationship. For example, I know a bipolar man who went out to a location to shoot a documentary and fell in love with the director. There was nothing for him to do about it; the object of his love was ten years younger than he, married, and not showing any interest in him. Nevertheless, he treasured the emotion because love is a wonderful thing.

At any time, you may feel love for a friend, a baby, a pet, or the woman ahead of you in the supermarket line. Just realize that love does not ensure that you can build any relationship with the one you care for.

I can't tell what my friend is feeling because he's a "tough guy" and doesn't show his feelings. How can I tell if he loves me?

A tough guy once told me, "Love hits me like a Mack truck." Don't worry too much if you have trouble reading his emotions. Ultimately, you may have to confront him and discuss how you both feel, but start out softly. Let your love come through when you are around him, and see if he will sense it and respond. If he doesn't, then hit him with the truck.

Aren't physical attraction and sex the most important parts of a relationship?

No. Love and the ability to be your true self around someone else are more important in relationships. Sex often seems to be the most important thing in the world to teenagers and people in the throes of mania. However, once you experience real love, sex pales by comparison.

SEX

Bipolar disorder can make sexual feelings increase or decrease during episodes just like emotions do. Individual experiences differ, but an abnormally high interest in sex is frequently seen in bipolar mania, whereas a decline in sex drive usually accompanies bipolar depression. These changes can make it hard to remain synchronized with your partner's sexual needs and expectations.

Lately, all my bipolar partner wants to do is have sex. Is this normal?

Uncontrolled mania can cause a person's sex drive to increase inappropriately without their awareness. Once I knew a bipolar manic Hollywood producer who came in with a sexual complaint. He said, "Wes, something is going wrong with my sex life. A month ago I used to have sex seven or eight times a day, but now I seem to have completely lost interest. Now I only need sex five times every day." Clearly, his level of sexual appetite was still abnormally exaggerated, but this individual failed to notice because his insight was impaired by mania.

How do I tell my friend that I only want to be held close and not have sex?

Your partner may have developed expectations about intimacy while your sex drive was artificially increased by bipolar disorder. If this is the case, inform your partner that you now need them to be romantic and caring rather than sexual. Tell them how you feel and exactly what you expect them to do.

How can I avoid being taken advantage of sexually?

Sexual exploitation happens all too frequently to bipolar individuals. When you are out in social situations, try to avoid doing anything that will cloud your judgment or stir up your bipolar illness, such as drinking, taking drugs, or staying up all night. Try to surround yourself with friends who respect you and like you for who you really are. Develop your natural caution. Instead of trusting everyone, let each person build up a track record of respectful, supportive, reliable, and honest behavior toward you.

Remember that you have no obligation to anyone but yourself. If someone is making you feel guilty for refusing to have sex with them or if they are pressuring you to take part in sexual practices that you do not approve of, they are being disrespectful and exploitive. You are empowered to make your own decisions for your own life.

Once I treated a bipolar woman whose problem was that she could not keep from giving men oral sex on the first date. She said, "They all want me to do it. I don't want to hurt their feelings." It is more important for you to run your own life than to cater to another person's desire for sex. People who try to take advantage of you are not worth holding on to. Whatever happens, hang on to your self-respect.

Why is my sexual behavior sometimes so uncharacteristic of me and my morals?

Uncontrolled bipolar disorder can make you act like another person. In particular, symptoms of impulsivity and hypersexuality can get you into situations you will regret. Alcohol makes things worse by further destabilizing your illness. Get your illness under better control if you want to preserve your personal values. Do not make yourself vulnerable to unplanned sex, exposure to disease, or social ridicule. If you have bipolar disorder, be safe, not sorry.

Q Should I discuss my sexual fantasies about other people with my spouse?

Before you discuss sexual fantasies that could potentially hurt your spouse or damage your marriage, you should first discuss them with your doctor and therapist. Make sure that you are thinking objectively and that your feelings are not being driven by bipolar disorder.

ANGER AND JEALOUSY

Bipolar disorder can make you vulnerable to anger outbursts or tantrums. However, if you are thinking of a long-term relationship with someone, it may be important that you behave honestly without trying to hide your true nature.

I knew a charming bipolar man who met and married his dream wife—a rich, famous Hollywood celebrity who loved him dearly. Out of fear for his relationship, he hid his terrible temper from her as long as he could. Finally, he lost control one day and his usual temper came out in a huge fight that caused a rift in their marriage. It seems that if his wife had known what to expect from the beginning, she might have been more understanding of his occasional bad temper. However, she never had a chance to see the real person, only the fake role he was always playing around her.

You could also avoid a lot of misery if you find a partner who is not so intimidated by a display of anger. If you are a good-hearted person, there are plenty of people who don't mind an emotional outburst every so often, as long as you come back to normal and don't hold a grudge. Let your loved ones see that you are making progress on anger in your treatment and they will be more understanding.

Q I'm just an irritable person. How can I keep from pushing loved ones away?

Just be yourself. Explain that it is your nature to be irritable sometimes but you always get over it quickly. Do not buy into the idea that something is wrong with you that you have to change; the problem is limited to your emotion and how you express it. Ask your therapist to help you work on reducing your experience and expression of negative emotions and ask your doctor to fine-tune your medications to minimize undue anger. Go to support groups and/or bipolar society meetings to research and discuss your particular irritability issues (see chapter 10, Resources).

Is bipolar disorder related to pathological jealousy?

I often see extreme jealousy in patients with bipolar disorder, especially during periods of mania. These jealous fits are commonly illogical, but they are often impossible to stop while someone is manic. When mania is present, medications need to be strengthened until the moment is past. When your thoughts are logical again, it is time to discuss the issue with your partner and your psychotherapist. You will be much happier when there is no longer jealousy in the air.

How can I keep from snooping on my significant other? I am always worried that there's someone else.

Change gears. Instead of worrying about whether you can trust someone, go by his or her track record. Have they been open, honest, and respectful throughout your relationship? Do they say and do things that remind you that your relationship is secure? Seek objective opinions from your doctor and therapist and work on developing your own objectivity. If someone has a history of disloyalty and disrespect, question why you are with them in the first place.

My spouse is really angry and won't have sex with me. Is this bipolar disorder?

Anger is one of the main reasons that people lose interest in sex with their partners. Other important causes of lost sexual interest include depression and alcohol use. All three—anger, depression, and alcohol use—can be augmented by bipolar disorder. If your spouse's anger does not subside in a timely way, try reasoning or negotiating, perhaps with the aid of a couples' therapist.

FANTASIES AND OBSESSIONS

One of the greatest challenges facing individuals with bipolar disorder is to stop intellectualizing and break the habit of fantasizing. Believe in the here and now, in what you can see and touch, and you will emerge victorious from emotional conflicts.

Q I know this relationship will work because I found someone who's perfect. That's great news, right?

Not necessarily. Everyone in the real world has both good points and faults, so if someone appears perfect, it is probably a fantasy inside your head. Your relationship will be more healthy and successful when you can see your friend for who he or she really is, both the good and the bad.

For example, I had great concern for one of my patients when he told me that his new girlfriend was "perfect." I knew that he was thinking of his girlfriend as a fantasy rather than seeing how she really was. It did not matter whether his fantasy was good or bad, optimistic or pessimistic; the fact that he was seeing the world in a distorted way made it hard for him to have a healthy relationship.

The relationship was rocky, but I knew things were better when my patient came in one day and said, "My girlfriend isn't perfect. She has lots of things I don't like but I can usually put up with them." This told me that my patient was out of his fantasy and able to deal with the real world. The couple went on to marry and have a good life together.

I've found the perfect partner, but he is married. Help!

If this person is married, then he is not the perfect partner for you. Turn your thoughts from your bipolar fantasies to the reality of the situation. Instead of obsessing about the married person, switch gears and look for someone else.

I can visualize relationships working great but then they fall apart in real life. Why?

Real relationships are never as good as their fantasy counterparts in your mind. Notice when you are fantasizing and try to limit your thoughts to what you know is true in the present. You will enjoy your life more when you get out of your head and start experiencing the real world around you.

Why does my partner want to leave our relationship when I think everything is great?

I once worked with a bipolar depressed woman who was amazed when she arrived home and found that her fiancé had left her and moved in with a twenty-year-old girl. We started her on mood stabilizers and, as she came back to her true self, she realized that this affair had been happening under her nose for a year but she could not see it because bipolar disorder was clouding her vision.

Bipolar disorder can blind us to the interpersonal events happening around us. This comes, in part, from the need for a grandiose fantasy that everything is going wonderfully. Individuals also frequently assume that other people react and feel like they do. Ask your partner what they are feeling and why; this may give you the information you need to find out what is going wrong.

Why do I sometimes become obsessed with new people I meet?

Obsession is a combination of recurrent, intrusive, unwanted thoughts and fantasies about how things will turn out in the future. Obsessions, left uncorrected, can sometimes sabotage a relationship. If you find that you are obsessing about a relationship, it is better to back off a bit from the relationship until your thoughts and judgment are clear again. If you cannot keep intrusive thoughts out of your mind, then check with your psychiatrist to make sure you are taking enough mood stabilizer(s) and other medicines that reduce recurrent thoughts. You will feel much better when your head is not full of obsessions.

I always keep wanting to call my ex but my friends warn me not to get involved again. Why do they say I was miserable when I just remember the good times?

People suffering from bipolar disorder often use a coping strategy called avoidance. After something unpleasant has happened, they try to push it out of their minds and make it disappear. This often leads people to get back into bad relationships. But, do not act hastily. Go to a support group or online forum and see if anyone else's relationship stories remind you of your past problems. Ask a friend or family member to help you review the problems that you had with your ex until you can remember them clearly. Then see if you still want to call.

SOCIAL BOUNDARIES IN RELATIONSHIPS

Social boundaries give us the ability to distinguish ourselves from others. In bipolar disorder, these boundaries may be so weak that you feel another person's pain or joy or depression as if it were your own. Boundary problems can make it difficult to be yourself around others.

Why is it that whenever I'm with somebody, all I can think about is what they think of me?

In bipolar disorder, weak social boundaries can make everyone's opinion of you seem like it is your own self-judgment, as if what they think determines who you are. You have to become self-sufficient and be able to retain your own sense of yourself distinct from others in order to have a healthy relationship. Make a habit to check periodically to see if you are listening to your own thoughts about yourself. Ask your psychotherapist to work with you on interpersonal "boundary issues." You will be glad you did.

Why do I always find myself doing anything possible to keep someone from leaving me?

In bipolar disorder, weak social boundaries can blur the distinction between yourself and others with whom you are close. In relationships, it can seem that two people's personalities are merged, as if the two of you had become one person. This experience may or may not be shared by your partner. Because of this merging, when someone threatens to leave it feels like they are taking a piece of you with them, leaving an empty hole. The solution to this problem is to disentangle yourself gradually from the other person until you can see the two of you as separate entities. You may begin this process by noticing, when you think of them, whether you are thinking of them as separate or merged with you. When they are merged, take a moment to separate them in your mind, until you can see yourself as a distinct personality. Your psychotherapist should be able to help you with this exercise.

Separation can be doubly difficult for bipolar individuals when the stress of relationship problems stirs up their bipolar illness. If the threat of separation has left you feeling overwhelmed and unable to think effectively, you may be vulnerable to an episode of mania or depression. Reduce your life stress, work with your psychotherapist, and ask your doctor to strengthen your medications until this stressful period is past.

Q I am a good friend but hearing everyone's problems makes me depressed. What do you suggest?

In bipolar disorder, the negative feelings of others can make such a great impression that they feel like your own feelings. You must be willing to make your own health your top priority even if that means that your friends will have to handle their own problems for a while. If you really want to help them, become a role model for your friends by keeping yourself happy and healthy. If their problems are just too complicated, ask them to consider going to a therapist, support group, or online forum (see chapter 10, Resources).

Q Why do the favors I do for other people always backfire? I'm just treating people like I would want to be treated.

Weakened social boundaries in bipolar disorder can make it seem that other people are just like you. Try to remember that helping people consists of doing things they want and not doing things you would want or things you think would be good for them. Usually it is best to wait until someone asks you for help. Then, if you feel like doing what is asked, you will know that you are really helping them.

I remember a bipolar man who met a woman for dinner on their first date. When his date arrived, she mentioned that she had been given a parking ticket outside the restaurant. The man thought about how much he would like other people to take care of his tickets and, despite her protestations, he insisted on going outside to the policeman and "fixing" the ticket. To his great surprise, when he returned to the restaurant he found that his date had called a cab and gone home. Although he meant well, he did something she did not like or want him to do.

I'm always calling and sending my special friend e-mails and cards and giving little presents, but we aren't getting any closer.

I realize that *you* would love to receive lots of e-mails, cards, and little presents from an admirer. However, it may come as a surprise to you that many people find the intense attention of bipolar individuals annoying. Back off a little bit and see if your friend warms up.

If I think my partner wants to break up with me, shouldn't I try to break up first?

It is easy in bipolar disorder to imagine that you are feeling the same as your partner does. If you are afraid they do not want you, it may occur to you to break up with them first. Unfortunately, lots of people with bipolar disorder lose close relationships this way that could have been saved. Do not give up so easily. If you want to keep the relationship, then talk to your partner about the problems in the relationship and discuss the issues with your psychotherapist. Most of all, decide what you really want and try to get it.

FINDING THE RIGHT PARTNER

My single bipolar patients ask more about finding and meeting new partners than almost any other issue. What with mood swings and changes in energy, sex drive, and sociability, it can be hard for people with bipolar disorder to find the right partner. However, do not give up. There are plenty of people out there who are quite compatible with you. You just have to find them.

Where can I go to find dates other than in bars? I don't like the people I meet there.

Bars are dangerous for bipolar individuals because alcohol can worsen bipolar symptoms. Successful places to meet nice people include special interest clubs, volunteer organizations, church or temple meetings, classes, and sports activities. For example, if you can play tennis at all, consider signing up for partners at your favorite tennis court. Activities like these can be a healthy, low-key, safe way to meet friendly people, and they are usually more fun than sitting around in a bar.

What do you think about meeting people over the Internet?

I think that the Internet is a fine place to meet and talk to people and build social skills, and many bipolar individuals find the online world comfortable. However, the amount and type of information you find out about people over the Internet is limited, and it may not be enough for you to decide if you want to meet someone in person. The Internet attracts predaceous, perverse, and undesirable characters that would usually be weeded out if they tried to meet you through healthy social encounters. For example, if your brother or sister gives your name to a friend, that person has already passed through several stages of social screening. Even though you hear stories of wonderful Internet relationships, I think that Internet dating is still too risky and too unlikely to generate good prospects for long-term relationships to recommend it to my bipolar patients.

I have a very specific idea of what kind of person I want to meet. How can I find someone who fits the profile?

Many bipolar individuals come to me with specific details like the ideal height, weight, age, hair, and eyes they want to find in a partner. However, you cannot use a shopping list to pick someone to share your life. First, you have to find someone that you care for and that cares for you. By that time, most of the personal details will have taken care of themselves.

Q Do I have to date? I'm looking for a long-term relationship and there's no point going out with someone who doesn't qualify.

The uncertainty of dating is anathema to lots of single people with bipolar disorder. Nevertheless, you often have to spend time looking for the right person, and going out with someone gives you a chance to enjoy spending a nice evening. Some people do not make a very good first impression, and it is important that you take time to get to know others before you make a decision about whether or not they are right for you. If you make some new friends, you may find that there are some you want to get close to.

Q Isn't it important that two people share the same hobbies and relaxation activities?

Everyone has heard this, but don't obsess about these details. Hobbies will not mean much when you have been together for ten or twenty years. Look for inner character and the ability to care about others.

Q Other than what they tell me, how else can I tell if somebody really cares for me?

Take a look at the way the other person treats you. Is he or she respectful, considerate, polite, and caring?

Q I always know exactly how I feel about
    somebody after thirty seconds. Why
    do some feel this is too soon?

Your feelings are real, but bipolar emotions can change easily and you
should know that relationships based on first impressions have a very poor
success rate. The shortest bipolar relationship I ever knew started with "in-
stant love" at a New Year's Eve party. There was sex and fun on New Year's
Day and the couple married the next morning. They began divorce pro-
ceedings before the end of the week.

Many couples who have had successful, long-term, loving relationships
say that it takes *at least* six months to get to know someone deeply.

STARTING NEW RELATIONSHIPS

The beginning of new relationships is a delicate time, when two people
grow to appreciate and respect each other. It is a time when individuals are
worried about saying or doing things that may distance themselves from
their new partner. The beginning of new relationships is also an opportunity to determine if you are compatible with your new partner and
whether they are the right one for you.

Q What should I do to make a really big impression
    on the new person I am dating?

I am sure that you are looking for someone who likes you as you are, not
for some show you put on. Just try to feel comfortable being yourself.

Q I met a great person and we've spent every minute together for the last week. How can I make sure it never stops?

Actually, things might work out better in the long run if you do not stick to each other like glue. Spending some time by yourself will increase your objectivity and give the relationship a chance to breathe. That way you will keep your relationship from burning out.

Q How I can tell my partner that I'm really not as outgoing and self-confident a person as I look?

Show your friend what you are like by acting like your own most natural self. If you are putting on an act of being happy, outgoing, self-confident, etc., then stop it. Give your friend a chance to like you for who you are.

Q Whenever I start dating someone, I always call all my friends to get their opinions. Is that a good idea?

There is no way that other people can know how *you* feel about someone. In addition, dates do not like it when they find out that their private affairs are being discussed by a bunch of other people. If you are not sure what to do, give the relationship more time until you know the other person better and you can be sure about your feelings.

Q Should I tell my new partner about my old
relationships? Won't that help my date
see that I'm honest and loyal?

My feeling is that it is not polite to discuss past relationships in front of anyone you are currently dating, even (or especially) if they bring up the topic
first. Stay in the present and let your date know that you think he or she is
special.

Q Should I tell my new partner what goes on
in my psychotherapy session?

Generally, I advise patients not to discuss their psychotherapy sessions with
others. What happens in your session is for you alone.

Q I have been dating this person for a month.
Should I tell them I have bipolar disorder?
I feel like I'm hiding something. I mean,
I'll have to tell them sometime, right?

Your personal health is really your own business and nobody else's. Usually,
those unaffected by the disorder have a hard time understanding it. If you
want to share this with your partner, do not hurry. Take time and wait for
the right moment or let the person bring it up. Invite your partner to get
this book to help learn about bipolar disorder. Above all, do not feel guilty
that you have bipolar disorder. You are a great person and you have nothing to confess.

I don't want to tell my partner I love him
    until he tells me first. Isn't that smart?

It is fine either to tell other people how you feel now or wait until you feel
more comfortable about discussing it. Just remember to be yourself and do
not play games.

How bad is it if my date talks to other people
    on the cell phone when we're out
    together?

Your friend should pay attention to you, but do not expect to be his or her
only concern in life. Forget the cell phone and ask yourself if you are being treated with respect and dignity in this relationship. Respect includes
consideration, attention, empathy, and refraining from hurtful speech and
action. Look inside yourself and see if you are being treated like a mature
adult of true inner worth. If you are not being treated with respect, walk
away.

My new friend is nice to me but is always
    rude to waiters in restaurants.
    What does that mean?

It tells you that your partner is willing to treat people disrespectfully. If your
partner treats others with disrespect, then be aware that he or she may treat
you in the same way. This is not a good predictor for future relationship potential.

What does it mean when my new friend keeps telling me bad stories about her ex? Is this an attempt to show that she likes me better?

One thing it means is that she is willing to treat other people in her life disrespectfully. Will she be talking that way about you someday?

What does it mean when someone dresses carelessly or inappropriately for our first date?

It is not a good sign. Your date could be disrespectful or just a slob. Bear in mind that not everyone has perfect social skills and you may have to tell the person you are dating specifically what you expect.

What should I make of the fact that my new boyfriend only wants to talk about himself?

At least you know what he is interested in. Himself.

What does it mean if the girl doesn't even offer to pay for her dinner?

It does not necessarily mean anything. I have heard of many "tricks" to tell if a person is thoughtful, including opening or unlocking doors, turning off cell phones, or offering to pay for things, but these are pretty worthless. It is important if a date seems haughty, entitled, or lacking in humility, but do not play silly mind games over your dinner, or you will probably get indigestion.

What do I do if I catch my friend lying? How can I ever be trusting again?

People with bipolar disorder are often surprised how much lying has become a cultural norm and a careless habit for many individuals. For example, casual remarks like, "Oh, you look pretty," or, "I agree with you entirely," are often made for the sake of conversation rather than from conviction. Even important comments like, "I only like blondes," or, "I want lots of children," can be made without much thought. Sometimes it helps to check with your friend to make sure they are serious about things they say. If they lie about critical issues and pretend they are telling the truth, then you know this is truly a problem.

How much can I believe someone when they tell me they want to settle down and have a family?

It is hard to tell what anyone means when they talk about future plans because the future is not here yet. Many things happen along the way that change what we think and do. In short, I would not take for granted anything your partner says about future plans. Look to see whether your partner is mature enough to develop a stable, consistent, and secure life. Consider his or her potential skills as a parent. Bring your friend in contact with babies, young children, and happily married friends and see your friend's reaction.

My partner is always telling me how good I look. Isn't that important for a relationship?

Compliments are nice, but you should not depend on the comments of others to support your sense of self-worth. Instead, find satisfaction from within yourself that is not dependent on what others say or do. It is too easy to find shallow people who hand out superficial compliments.

Q I have been seeing this guy and I like him a lot, but he never tells me that he worships me or that I'm the most wonderful person he's ever seen. What's wrong?

His feelings may be sincere even if he does not think that you are godlike. Unless you really are the most wonderful person in the world, focus on what is truly important. Let him see that you are a self-sufficient, caring, and good-hearted person and be content with his admiration and respect.

Q Are there social and dating things I should watch out for when I'm sort of manic?

There are certain things you can do to be sure you are not taken advantage of and that you do not take advantage of others when you date, including:

- Be yourself.
- Do not be an actor or entertainer.
- Do not drink, use drugs, or do anything that will cause you to lose control.
- Do not spend a lot of money.
- Avoid getting intimate with anyone for the first time when you are manic.
- Make all your own decisions and take your time.
- If you start to feel uncomfortable or out of control when you are out, make some excuse, and go home immediately.

DON'T GET HURT BY OTHER PEOPLE

Sometimes subtle meanings and emotional tones can be hurtful to a depressed person, whereas someone who is not depressed might shrug off the same comments. On the other hand, I have also seen plenty of depressed persons treated in a disrespectful, hurtful way. Either way, it should be a goal of your bipolar treatment to make you less vulnerable to being hurt, whether you are sensitive or not.

Every time I get into a relationship, I end up getting hurt. Am I sabotaging myself?

Oftentimes, children growing up with bipolar disorder fail to learn to recognize subtle, social nuances. As adults, they may find it difficult to weed out potential partners who are selfish, untrustworthy, or insincere. It may be challenging for them to express caring emotions without becoming too intense or obsessive and pushing away the ones they care for.

Take advantage of others' experience in these areas. Talk with friends and family about how they handle relationship issues in their lives. Read other bipolar people's relationship stories online and figure out where they succeeded and failed. Find a support group or online forum where you can talk about social relationships freely (see chapter 10, Resources). Ask your therapist to work with you on social communication and intimacy and help you get rid of any maladaptive social habits you may have picked up over the years.

Is it possible that someone could try to take advantage of me when I'm manic or depressed?

Yes. You may be vulnerable to someone who wants to take advantage of you for sex, money, drugs, company, a boost in self-image, or as someone to control, pick on, or take responsibility for their own misdeeds. It is easy to tell when persons with bipolar disorder are vulnerable, and many people prey on this vulnerability.

Why is my partner great when we are alone but very distant when we're around other people?

There are lots of possible explanations for this behavior. Maybe your partner is shy or embarrassed if you act loud and boisterous. An unlikely reason

---

A BIPOLAR GOLDEN RULE: HELP OTHER PEOPLE KEEP FROM HURTING YOU

. . . .

Most individuals will feel sorry if they victimize you, and will feel bad about themselves later. Through the years, guilty memories and self-recrimination can accumulate until they become a great burden. By being less vulnerable to others, you are protecting yourself and also protecting other people from remorse later on.

---

could be that your partner is ashamed to be seen with you. Talk to your partner and see if you can find out what he or she is thinking.

I've fallen in love with a professor who's helping me, and we're having sex. How do I hook him?

You do not want to hook him. Just be your most natural self and if there is good compatibility, the two of you will come together. You should know, however, that there is an imbalance of power in relationships with teachers, therapists, physicians, etc., that can contribute to unhealthy relationships, stress, and being taken advantage of socially, sexually, and/or materially.

What does it mean that my new friend never wants me to meet his other friends?

I wonder if your friend is hiding them from you or you from them. You could be imagining a motive that is not really there. Discuss your concerns with your new friend and bring it up in your psychotherapy sessions.

I keep giving my friends second chances but
they keep doing things that hurt me.
What can I do?

Make sure you are able to tell your friends exactly what you need from
them and be sure they understand. Ask yourself if you are being too trusting and use your psychotherapy sessions to try and figure out what is going
on. In the meantime, you may have to distance yourself from your friends
until you can tolerate their company again.

My boyfriend had an affair with my best friend
but he says it was only his bipolar disorder
and he was out of control. Should I believe
him and take him back?

It depends on how hard he is working to bring his bipolar disorder under
control. If his illness is not well controlled, you can expect this incident to
repeat itself. Also, look back and see what has happened when you have
given him second chances before. People are usually consistent.

I trusted my friend with my money and then
my friend cheated me. I'm so hurt.

Do not be so trusting that you make it easy for others to take advantage of
you. Many people lose money when their bipolar disorder is unstable. If
your illness is acting up, get your doctor to help make it stable again.

I introduced my best friend to a guy I had
a crush on. Then my friend took him
away from me.

Never do this. I hear this a lot in my discussions with bipolar patients. Sometimes the bipolar person encourages the friendship or even sets up dates for the couple. People tell me that they want all their friends to be happy, but they end up cheating themselves. Remember that you are not a social director, and it is not your job to pair up your friends. The solution is this: do not promote relationships for anyone that you want to keep for yourself.

I seem to spend more time helping other
people than I spend helping myself.
Why is that?

I see this happen frequently in bipolar disorder. There is often a tendency to help everybody and ensure their well-being at the expense of your own. This may be driven by bipolar overdependence on what others think of you or fantasies that you will be their savior. Just remember that you are probably a good person and you deserve a good life. Do not be afraid to put yourself and your future first.

I feel used by dates who are always after me
to buy them things and spend money
on them. I can't say "No."

It is often hard to say no in bipolar disorder, especially if you are bullied or made to feel selfish. This feeling can be worsened if you are filled with bipolar self-doubt or overdependence on what others think of you. You can always tell these needy people that you have changed your mind, or just do not do what they ask. Even better, you can choose to stay away from people who want things from you. Meanwhile, ask your family, friends, and/or therapist to help you role-play saying no in these situations. Talk on the Internet with other bipolar individuals who have had similar experiences. Try to decide what you are willing to do for other people in advance and do not change your mind when people ask for more.

My boyfriend is hurt that I won't lend him any more money. Can I trust him?

Actually, I do not recommend that people with bipolar disorder lend money. I have seen too many people with uncontrolled bipolar disorder throw away fortunes in a few months. Instead, focus on staying healthy and let your boyfriend take care of his own money problems.

I like to show people I'm generous. If I give my new girlfriend a car, will she take me seriously?

If your gift giving is inappropriate, the recipient may be put off. Instead of expensive material gifts, try offering your patience, respect, and caring, and see if she responds in kind.

Giving inappropriately extravagant gifts is a well-known phenomenon in mania. Check with your doctor, friends, and family to make sure you are thinking logically. If you are showing manic signs, go to your doctor and discuss how to improve your health.

NOW THAT I'M MYSELF AGAIN

After you have bounced back from bipolar illness, it is time to settle back into a normal life and stable, rewarding relationships. Here are a few tricks for making the transition.

Why doesn't my partner like me now that I have my bipolar disorder under control?

Partners are often drawn to bipolar individuals whose mania makes them entertaining, outgoing, sociable, decisive, and self-assured. Sometimes partners are drawn to individuals with bipolar depression because depressed individuals are vulnerable, noncompetitive, and easy to control. Now that you are well, you have to focus on being yourself. I am sure that there are many things to like about you that do not have anything to do with your bipolar disorder. If your partner cannot see your desirable qualities, you can point them out directly or in counseling. Ultimately, if they cannot appreciate you, dump them.

When I was manic, I wanted sex all the time. Now that I am no longer manic, my partner feels cheated. Do you have any advice?

It is easy to fall in love with someone's mania when they are upbeat and sexy. Moreover, when individuals are manic, their sex drives high, and their thinking clouded, they are perfect targets to be taken advantage of by the opposite sex. Make it clear to your mate that the mania is gone for good and you are a different, healthier person now. Then you can invite your partner to start your relationship again with the real you.

My doctor's upset because my spouse keeps trying to sabotage my treatment. What's going on?

Spouses have actually contacted me and asked me to make their partners manic or depressed again. I can only assume that these spouses do not appreciate how heartbreaking bipolar disease can be.

Q I dated and married my spouse while I was sick
with bipolar disorder but now I'm well
and I don't think I love him anymore.
What do I do?

He may have behaved badly during your bipolar episode or he may not be
as good as you thought he was. Nevertheless, there is often a core of deep
caring between people who have stayed together during a crisis. See if you
can discover this core and nurture it. Your friends, family, and/or therapist
may be able to help you see how you are good together. You may find that
the two of you have a mature, loving relationship after all.

SEVEN RULES FOR SAFE
BIPOLAR DATING

1. Always arrange your own transportation and meet your date in a
   neutral place. If you feel uncomfortable then you can always leave.
2. Do not go to someone's home or let them come to yours until you
   have known that person for several months.
3. Make sure that the time and activity of dates are planned in advance. Refuse to do things at the last minute; this is disrespectful to
   you and a common tool of those who want to take advantage.
4. Refuse to talk about topics that make you feel uncomfortable or are
   too personal. As a rule, it is impolite for others to ask personal questions and there is no need for you to answer them.
5. If you aren't treated with respect or are expected to do anything
   that you do not want to do, leave immediately.
6. Do not drink, stay up late, or have sex with anyone when you start
   dating them. Ideally, wait as long as possible.
7. When starting a relationship, do not call or visit your partner every
   day. Once or twice a week is better.

8

WOMEN'S ISSUES IN BIPOLAR DISORDER

. . . .

I believe it is important to devote a section of this book solely to bipolar women and their own special challenges. Bipolar disorder occurs more frequently in women, and the physical illness directly affects the female body. Bipolar disorder interacts with female hormones and the menstrual cycle and plays a role in issues of pregnancy, sex, and relationships.

BIPOLAR PREMENSTRUAL SYNDROME

Over the years, I have been impressed with the misery that many women with bipolar disorder experience during their menstrual cycle. Women with bipolar disorder are especially vulnerable to menstrual mood swings, anger, and depression that can be incapacitating.

Why does my PMS last for two weeks a month when every other woman's lasts only a few days?

In most women, premenstrual symptoms are limited to a day or two before the start of menses. However, many women with bipolar disorder experience physical and emotional symptoms, as well as breakthrough bipolar symptoms, for as many as two weeks per month. As one of my patients put it: "PMS is half of my life." This may improve with the medical treatment needed to control bipolar disorder or additional steps may have to be taken.

What is the most common effective treatment for PMS?

Taking a nonsteroidal anti-inflammatory drug (NSAID) relieves common menstrual symptoms for most women. You already know many over-the-counter medicines in this group, such as Motrin and Advil. Anaprox (naproxen) is a prescription NSAID that has a high rate of satisfaction among women with PMS. Supplement this by avoiding salt and lying down if possible: both promote mild diuretic effects that can help reduce the fluid retention that is common in PMS.

Spironolactone (Aldactone) is a molecular copy of a natural body diuretic, which can successfully reduce PMS in many bipolar women. It may even have mild mood-stabilizing effects. Ask your doctor about it.

My friends take herbs for PMS. Do they work and are they safe?

Other than NSAIDs, the safety and efficacy of over-the-counter preparations for PMS in bipolar women is unclear. Stay away from preparations that contain hormones or hormone-like substances. Also, avoid over-the-counter combination products that contain stimulants—these will do more harm than good.

My other doctor said that antidepressants could treat PMS. Is this safe for bipolar women?

Taking antidepressants can destabilize bipolar disorder and even make it permanently worse. Therefore, I do not recommend that you take antidepressants for PMS.

Q I heard somewhere that lithium salt will also
    treat my PMS. Is this true?

Lithium salt, which is both a mood stabilizer and a diuretic, was listed in older medical literature as a treatment for PMS. I have cared for many women taking lithium as a treatment for bipolar disorder, but many of them still had premenstrual problems.

Q I suffer from my wife's PMS every month.
    Can you give her something so she
    won't be such a pain?

PMS is no joke. You could look at it another way. Men get a break every month because they do not have to menstruate.

PREGNANCY

Because bipolar disorder may be transferred genetically, bipolar women often wonder if they should have children. I think the answer is yes. It is quite possible that your children will not get the gene for bipolar disorder. Even if they do, I think that the next generation of children born to well-educated, bipolar parents will be in much better mental health than any generation before them. This will be the first generation where parents with bipolar disorder will be making sure that their children get effective treatment at the first signs of the disease. I expect that this will minimize the life-time severity of symptoms in these children and allow them to develop their own special talents to the fullest. I can hardly wait to see it happen.

Q I can't function without my medications. Will
    they damage the baby if I get pregnant?

Some medications are more dangerous than others, and it is often possible to switch to safer ones if you are pregnant. There are many medications with mood-stabilizing effects. Our understanding of the effects of medications on pregnancy is constantly being updated. When you are ready to get pregnant, have an extensive talk with your psychiatrist to find out the current state of the art.

It is not a safe solution to discontinue your medications while pregnant and simply hope for the best. If you have bipolar disorder, there are risks if you take medications and risks if you do not. For example, persons with unmedicated bipolar disorder have more serious accidents, including motor vehicle accidents, which could endanger the baby. Women who are sick with bipolar disorder are more likely to be poorly nourished and may make impulsive decisions that could endanger themselves and their unborn children. Stress hormone levels are higher in untreated bipolar disorder, and some doctors believe these high stress hormone levels can harm early fetal development. When you are ready, check your resources, do your research, and make your mind up as to which options are the best choice for you.

What bipolar drugs are harmful and which are safe in pregnancy?

Our assessment of the risks and benefits of bipolar medications in pregnancy changes every year. Every year also brings the introduction of a raft of new medicines for bipolar disorder as well as new research and treatment options. The thing to do is to wait until you are ready to become pregnant and then look at the newest research and treatments available.

What should I do when I decide I'm ready to get pregnant?

When you decide you are ready for pregnancy, get your psychiatrist, obstetrician, and family doctor or internist together to discuss your bipolar treatment. Divide your nine-month pregnancy into weeks and try to come up with a weekly nine-month plan covering all contingencies for your health and your baby's safety. For example, if you become depressed at five months you should already have figured out what you will do (like start lamotrigine or another medication), and have another backup plan if the first plan fails. After your nine-month plan is in place, you and your caretakers will know what to do for every eventuality and you can relax. Remember that psychotherapy is not risky to your new baby. As long as you are thinking clearly, reality-based, interpersonal, cognitive, and/or behavioral therapies can help reduce symptoms.

Does bipolar disorder make it more likely that I will become depressed after my son is born?

There are two types of "depression" that follow the birth of a child. The first is called "baby blues," and it occurs during the first week or so after birth. It is a period of emotional discomfort, but it usually does not meet the official diagnostic criteria for true clinical depression. This condition probably has nothing to do with bipolar disorder.

Postpartum depression is a true, clinical depression that may start up to four weeks after birth and can last for weeks or months. Postpartum depression occurs mostly in bipolar women, where it resembles usual bipolar depression. I always advocate being prepared. This bipolar depression is often severe and it comes at a time when a mother needs to be psychologically and physically healthy in order to care for her newborn baby.

The solution to postpartum depression is medication treatment. If you have stopped your bipolar medications during pregnancy, resume them as soon as possible. Some knowing physicians have them on hand in the birthing suite so they can be given immediately after birth. This can help prevent postpartum depression from ever beginning.

WOMEN'S SEXUAL ISSUES

You have a right to a fulfilling sex life and you should have one. Here are some of the sexual issues other bipolar women have faced after they brought their illness under control.

How can I get what *I* want from my sexual relationship? I'm always too concerned about trying to make sure the man gets what he wants.

Do not be too concerned about the other person and not concerned enough about yourself. I see this happening far too often in bipolar disorder. Do not be afraid to stand up for yourself. Explain to your partner explicitly what you want and need from them.

Can I have an orgasm if I am on medications for bipolar disorder?

In stark contrast with antidepressants, mood stabilizers usually do not cause problems with female sexual function. Some of my patients take their carbamazepine before having sex because they say it helps them relax.

Actually, it is common for women with bipolar depression to begin having orgasms for the first time when their bipolar disorder comes under control. If you have been suffering from bipolar depression and you are unable to achieve orgasms—especially if you have had them before—then give yourself a chance, relax, and I am sure they will return. It takes a while to recover fully from depression. If your beliefs permit it, you can also learn a lot about your body by exploring your own sexuality. Many women have their first orgasm with a vibrator of some type. On the practical side, you should know that these are readily available for a few dollars, without guilt or embarrassment, at the nearest drugstore in the guise of muscle massagers.

I am middle-aged, recovered from depression, and I finally want sex again but now I can't lubricate. Should I take hormones?

I think it is safer and more reasonable just to use lubricants. Most women prefer water-based lubricants over greasy petroleum jelly. If you like, you can insert these discreetly before sex or you can apply them directly to your partner during foreplay. If your genital tissues have become thin, you can ask your doctor for low-potency topical hormone cream so that your body is exposed to the lowest possible hormone dose.

My sex interest has changed drastically in the last six months. Is bipolar disorder to blame?

Bipolar disorder often causes the sex drive to increase dramatically during mania, decrease during depression, and normalize when bipolar disorder is stabilized.

When I was manic, my sex drive was great but now I could care less. Should I stop the medications?

First, make sure you are not depressed, as this could be the root of your problem. Then, give yourself a chance to explore intimacy without mania. It will feel different, but you might like it better. If you surround yourself with those you love, your sexual drive will probably appear in its own time.

If you are recovering from bipolar disorder, you may have to rediscover how much sex feels normal for you. Chances are that it will be different from what you see on television and in movies. It probably will not fit your partner's sexual fantasies, either. Try to find your own most natural self. I think you will like what you find.

Last year I got a reputation for sleeping around because of my bipolar disorder. I don't do that anymore but everyone still treats me like crap. What do other girls do when this happens?

It is a tough situation. You have changed but people are not seeing that you have changed. In addition, you may know some immature people who enjoy making others miserable. When this happens during high school, things sometimes become so difficult that it becomes necessary to change schools.

If you want other people to know that you have changed, try to be your most natural, healthy self around them. Find friends who will accept you for the good person that you are and stick with them.

I went off my medications and I hooked up with my best friend's boyfriend. Once I went back on my meds, I was horrified at what I'd done, but my friend will not even talk to me. Have I lost her?

Possibly. It depends on how good a friend she is and how much the relationship is worth to you. Try explaining that you were not acting like yourself and ask for another chance. Tell her that you will show her that you can be a good and respectful friend. Then do it. If she will not agree, give her some time and tell her again.

I'm married, but I think my sexual orientation may be changing. Can this be due to bipolar disorder?

If you decide that you have discovered your true sexual orientation, then so be it. However, keep in mind that bipolar disorder causes fluctuations in sexual feelings and people with bipolar disorder often question their own sexuality. Give your feelings time to mature naturally and things will work out on their own.

I don't care about relationships. I just like the thought of sexual conquest. I love the chase.

That's fine, but please note that it may not help you find and develop a caring relationship with a potential life partner.

HORMONE SUPPLEMENTATION

Some authorities suggest that adding estrogen to other bipolar medications can improve their effectiveness. I have seen this in my own patients. However, estrogen supplementation is not safe enough to justify its use for this purpose alone. The medical risks and benefits of estrogen and progesterone supplementation have been a hot topic of argument for years. Check with your gynecologist and do some research on the Internet to find out the latest information.

What's the effect of progesterone on women with bipolar disorder?

I have observed progesterone bring on suicidal depression in bipolar women on several occasions. Medroxyprogesterone (Depo-Provera) is an example of a common, very long-acting form of progesterone that is often administrated as an intramuscular injection. If you have to decide about getting a progesterone shot, try taking a short-acting oral form of progesterone first to see how you feel. When I have given my female patients a low-dose progesterone tablet to try before they committed to progesterone therapy, none of them ever wanted to continue. A few of my patients have taken micronized progesterone (Prometrium) without severe problems, but I cannot guarantee that it is safe.

I've seen herbal extracts that claim to have estrogen. Is this true?

Many plants contain mixtures of phytoestrogens and phytosteroids with a variety of hormonal effects. The composition and potency of over-the-counter concentrates, extracts, and combination products varies. The benefits and risks for bipolar disorder are unknown, so I advise staying away from these products.

One of the most heinous products promoted for women's health is the extract of the Mexican wild yam (*Dioscorea* species). Legitimate drug companies use this herb to extract stress steroid hormones and male sex hormones that can exacerbate bipolar disorder if used improperly. I have observed agitation, anxiety, depression, and psychosis in bipolar women patients after they mistakenly took Mexican wild yam extract they bought from health-food stores.

Will hormone supplements affect how I look?

Maybe. Generally, estrogens will make your tissues hold more water that may fill out facial wrinkles or make your clothes tight, depending on your body form. Progesterones may cause acne, hair loss, and muscular enlargement.

Every oral contraceptive I looked up has some type of estrogen and progesterone in it. What should I do about birth control?

It is especially important for women with bipolar disorder to plan their pregnancies in order to take care of issues like drug effects on the developing child. Discuss this with your gynecologist or family doctor. You may prefer to use other effective methods of contraception, like condoms, an IUD, or a diaphragm.

BIPOLAR WOMEN IN ABUSIVE RELATIONSHIPS

Many bipolar women are vulnerable to sexual or physical abuse, especially before their disorder is properly managed and treated. Just remember that you have a right to do (or not do) whatever suits you in a relationship. If you are not sure if you are in an abusive relationship, play it safe and get out. You can always reassess your situation when you are feeling better.

Q I respected my husband when I was depressed, but now that I am healthy, he acts like a spoiled little kid. What do you recommend?

It is an unfortunate fact that many men want their wives to mother them. If your husband reverted to childhood while your bipolar disorder was active, be reassured that these habits can be reversed. Treat your spouse like a mature adult and then insist that he do the same toward you.

Q My husband hit me while I was depressed. Could I have unintentionally elicited this behavior?

No matter what happened between the two of you, your husband does not have the right to use violence. You need to reassess your situation seriously to make sure it will never happen again. If you or your children are unsafe, then take them and leave immediately. Go to a friend or family member's home or look in the local telephone book for a battered women's helpline. Look on the Internet for resources and help for family violence. In this case, your primary responsibility is the safety of you and your children.

Q While I was manic, my husband talked me into throwing away most of my inheritance on stupid projects. What can I do?

First, do not give him any more money. Consider talking to your attorney to see if you can recoup any of your losses.

Under the influence of mania, many spouses are convinced to go along with get-rich-quick schemes, inappropriately costly purchases, and worse. Do not let this happen to you. If your bipolar disorder is temporarily out of control, seek advice from your doctor, therapist, family, and friends before you make major decisions or lifestyle changes.

Q My husband complains that I won't have sex with him anymore now that my bipolar disorder is controlled. He tells me that I must perform my marital duty.

Get your husband to come down to earth, please! You cannot be forced into having sex with a man just because he married you. Your husband will fare better if he tries caring and understanding instead of being pushy. It would probably help if he tried to be more likable and attractive to you as well. You can tell him I said so.

Q My forty-year-old bipolar wife used to go out late, party, get drunk, and have fun all the time, but after the medications she only wants to work and spend time at home with our children. What can I do to get my fun-loving wife back again?

I say, consider yourself fortunate to have a wife who can handle a career and her home life at the same time. Meanwhile, grow up and shoulder some responsibility. Life is not a big party.

Q Isn't the role of the wife to spend her time helping her husband?

In my opinion, as a woman struggling with bipolar disorder, your first "duty" as a wife is to keep yourself healthy, uphold your values, work to realize your goals, and share your love.

9

CRISIS MANAGEMENT: HOW FAMILY MEMBERS CAN HELP PREVENT CRISES

. . . .

Bipolar disorder is a disease of contrasts. Periodically things get worse. Our best defense against crises is to prepare for them in advance. Unfortunately, it takes a lot of work and practice to predict when bipolar disorder is taking a downturn. Once an exacerbation is in progress, it will be difficult for the patient to be objective about themselves or their condition. It is during this time that families can help their bipolar family member understand what is happening to them and direct them to the appropriate care.

SPOUSES, PARTNERS, AND FRIENDS

Everyone wants their loved ones to be healthy in mind, emotions, and spirit. It may be difficult to watch a loved one's progress when their illness is getting worse. My most frequent question from relationship partners is "What can I do?"

How can I help my loved one cope with his or her bipolar disorder?

There are two things you can do that are so important that they eclipse everything else. Encourage your bipolar partner to go to doctor's appointments and to take medications. Without these two elements, a bipolar treatment plan has no chance of working. Beyond this, your options become limited. The next best thing is to listen and provide emotional support. You are not the therapist or the doctor, so avoid taking over those roles. You cannot physically force your partner to go to appointments or take medications. Ultimately, the effort has to be their own. Make sure that they understand that if their bipolar disorder gets too far out of control, it may endanger the relationship you share.

How can I participate in my loved one's treatment?

Some doctors and patients will allow you to come to one or more of their appointments. I welcome partners to come in by themselves to learn about bipolar disorder and develop strategies to cope with their loved one's illness. Occasionally, I will see both partners together in couple's therapy.

Learn all you can about bipolar disorder. There are national and professional organizations with informative websites and local activities, including support groups. Some publish informative newsletters, magazines, and e-zines. Go to national and local meetings and lectures on bipolar disorder and get to know some of the bipolar community. Participate in online chat, bulletin boards, and Internet support groups and address your questions to other partners of bipolar persons. Get more ideas from Resources, chapter 10.

WARNING SIGNS

Sometimes you have to use your intuition and your knowledge of your loved one to figure things out. If they are not acting like themselves or the situation feels like it did before your loved one's last breakdown, then things are probably getting worse. Common signs of an impending bipolar crisis include:

- The onset of nocturnal insomnia
- The inability to read or watch a television program because of distractibility
- Sudden increased or decreased energy
- Sudden change of interests and activities

Can people make themselves manic on purpose?

I have known many individuals who have tried to keep themselves in a constant state of mania by drinking alcohol and coffee, taking drugs, staying up all night, working around the clock, or even increasing their stress levels by becoming embroiled in disagreements and emergencies. Eventually they crash into a bad depression.

If your loved one is engaging in activities that could promote mania, ask them to try to stop for a month and see what happens. If you think that the situation is getting out of hand, try to get your friend into the hospital, where multiple problems can be treated. My experience is that it is easier to treat the myriad problems of bipolar disorder in a hospital psychiatric ward than it is to treat bipolar disorder in a medical ward or substance abuse unit.

What can I do if I'm sure my husband is manic but he won't agree to go to the doctor? Can you help me?

You can offer to help your husband get to the psychiatrist for assessment and treatment. However, if your husband does not want treatment, you cannot help him.

Lately my bipolar husband has been spending all our food money buying expensive things we don't need. Where will this end?

It is likely to end with you and your family facing financial disaster. Get your spouse into the hospital. You may wish to take your husband's name off bank accounts and credit cards that you share and contact your attorney. Do not let your husband's illness hurt him and your family.

My wife says her mania will go away on its own and we should wait. Do you think that is wise?

If left alone, mania will often but not always go away on its own within three to six months. However, the process of mania is very damaging to work and personal relationships, bank accounts, and family well-being. It is often followed by bipolar depression. The question is, what will be left if you wait for nature to take its course?

My loved one's behavior is becoming extreme. How can I reason with him?

You may have to refer this problem back to your loved one's doctor and/or therapist. If your loved one's thinking is unclear, you may not be able to fix things by yourself and it may provoke a big fight if you try. Bipolar episodes often impair normal insight into one's actions, and your loved one may not be able to understand why their behaviors seem excessive. For example, a patient of mine became manic one spring, bought one hundred azalea bushes for a great sum, and squeezed them all into his tiny front yard. This seemed perfectly sensible to him at the time. No one could reason with him, because he had the whole thing figured out "logically." When he recovered, his family showed him the front yard crowded with bushes and he could not figure out why he had done this.

My brother is sure he can tell when he is getting manic. Can't he just take medications then?

Waiting to start medications does not work because nobody can tell reliably when they are getting manic. Even with all my experience, I could not tell if I was getting manic. It takes a professional experienced in bipolar disorder working closely with the patient to tell.

There was an interesting research study on this question. Bipolar individuals were taken off their medications and partnered with a caseworker who watched them closely. The caseworker held the medication and, at the first sign of mania, immediately gave it to the patient. It turned out that this group had just as many bipolar episodes and just as many hospitalizations as patients who never took any medication at all. Waiting until symptoms start to take the medication does not work.

For twenty years, we've been giving money to our manic son and we're broke. What do we do now?

I have heard this story too many times. Do not keep making the same mistakes over and over; it will not help you or your son. If you have proved that your son does not get better when you give him money, then stop and do something else. He can get professional treatment and medications at very low or no cost. Maybe you should insist that your son be seeing a doctor consistently and taking a regular, adequate dose of a mood stabilizer *before* you consider giving him any more money.

My bipolar wife cries for five or six hours every day and I can't console her. What is going on?

Generally, it is impossible to console somebody with bipolar depression because the problem is with inner, physiological systems and not with outside problems. Get your spouse to a bipolar specialist as soon as possible and encourage her to engage in her treatment. Go to mental health websites and learn more about bipolar disorder. Try going to a mental health association meeting or online support group and learning how other family members addressed this problem. If the situation is too severe, investigate hospitalization. There's not much else you can do until she begins to come back to herself again.

Q My husband has become so depressed that he
has stopped talking completely. What
do I do?

When bipolar individuals stop talking, we call it elective mutism. If your husband stops moving spontaneously, then the condition may be called catatonia. Decades ago, catatonia was thought to be restricted to schizophrenia, but now we know it is usually bipolar in origin. These syndromes are usually a sign of severe psychophysiological problems. Get your loved one to a doctor or hospital for a physical and psychiatric checkup.

Q Now my daughter flies into a rage at the least
provocation. Is her bipolar disorder
getting worse?

When emotional control becomes more difficult on the outside, it is often a sign that bipolar disorder is getting worse on the inside. Seek treatment. If violence is an issue, it may be necessary to hospitalize her where she can be watched carefully to alleviate the possibility of harm to herself or others.

Q My friend has become completely
withdrawn lately. Could this be
worsening bipolar disorder?

Frequently, persons with bipolar disorder will withdraw and become un-communicative before a psychotic break.

PSYCHOSIS

Psychosis is the most severe stage of bipolar disorder. Psychosis refers to a condition where a person is not able to discriminate external reality from internal experiences. Properly used, the word psychotic refers to any lapses of reality, but in practice many professionals use the word psychotic to denote the presence of hallucinations. The National Institute of Mental Health has published a useful list of psychotic symptoms that may be found in appendix B.

Reality is one of those concepts that is simple to understand but difficult to define. I once worked in a hospital ward where the nursing definition of psychiatric illness was "poor reality testing," and I think that this was a wise distinction. All of us are constantly checking to confirm that our beliefs about the world match the real world around us. In psychosis, people begin to doubt their normal worldview and suddenly anything is possible and fantasy becomes reality. This concept is a lot easier to understand if you have seen real psychosis (or experienced it yourself).

What are the most common kinds of psychotic experiences in bipolar disorder?

Common psychotic experiences in bipolar disorder include the belief that you are omnipotent, invulnerable, and godlike or that rules do not apply to you (grandiosity), the belief that others are plotting to harm you (paranoia), the experience of hearing voices (auditory hallucinations) or seeing things that are not there (visual hallucinations), and a belief in stories and facts that are not evident (delusions).

Can people act normal and be psychotic at the same time?

Frequently people will experience a lapse of reality yet appear normal from the outside. Sometimes acting secretive, conspiratorial, or alluding to mysterious sources of information provides a clue to this condition. Be advised that most people who are psychotic do not know it themselves, so do not be misled if they assure you they are fine.

The doctor said my wife was psychotic but she looks like she always does. Could he be wrong?

Frequently people reveal unrealistic beliefs or experiences in the safety of the psychiatrist's office that do not surface anywhere else. Many bipolar women and men I have seen had delusional misconceptions about themselves that they never aired in public. Other patients may confide their fears that others are out to get them, can read their minds, or have some special knowledge of them that is not consistent with reality. The psychiatrist may not be able to tell you specifically what is going wrong without violating the confidentiality of his or her patient.

What is a hallucination?

Hallucinations are the presence of any well-formed sensory information that is not in evidence. Hallucinations can involve hearing (auditory), seeing (visual), tasting (gustatory), touching (tactile), or smelling (olfactory). These can take the forms of hearing sounds, hearing voices, seeing illusory visions, feeling insects crawling on the skin, and so forth.

Are hallucinations ever normal?

I think so. Almost everyone has experienced benign hallucinations, although our culture does not encourage talking about them. For example, many people have heard noises or voices calling them in an empty house only to look and find that no one is there. Many people experience ringing in their ears (tinnitus), which is the hallucination of a sound that is not there. Most everyone has seen colors or shapes while their eyes are closed just before entering sleep. We commonly experience many other examples of benign hallucinations that are not caused by any mental or emotional problems.

I've started seeing blood and guts and people getting killed. Are you familiar with this?

I call this "horror movie hallucination" and I have observed it several times in bipolar disorder. It is as if a scene is superimposed over what you are naturally hearing and seeing and you cannot get it to stop. For example, a knife may be seen falling from the sky and chopping a nearby man's head off. Or a scene of battle and torture appears as if you are viewing everything through a war movie. It is a product of the brain imbalance in bipolar disorder and usually resolves with mood stabilizers or antipsychotics.

My husband has become so suspicious of me. Is he paranoid?

Possibly. In bipolar disorder, paranoia is usually a combination of feeling frightened by others (the sense that other people are against you) and beliefs that explain the details of the danger, usually in a dramatic story. You need to question him or call his doctor to make sure that he is not developing a paranoid delusion.

The doctor told me that my husband was delusional. What's that mean exactly?

A delusion is a belief that conditions are present and events are happening that have no basis in fact. Delusions can be simple, like the belief of a starving anorexic that he is overweight despite what he sees in the mirror. Delusions can also be complex, like the belief that the FBI is following someone because that person has some top secret information. A very common delusion in bipolar disorder is the belief that one is a very important person. Nowadays, people may believe they are a celebrity, a general, a confidant to the president, or a member of the FBI or CIA. During Napoleon's popularity in France, psychotic persons commonly held the delusion that they were Napoleon. Frequently the psychotic person believes they are involved in a complex and important plot. The source of these delusions are the feelings of grandiosity that are produced by the brain during psychotic bipolar disorder.

Sometimes rational people who are unfamiliar with psychosis are pulled into a psychotic person's delusions because they seem so impossible to make up. A proper evaluation will show if someone you care for has delusional bipolar disorder. Delusional individuals need to get treatment immediately in order to protect themselves and their families from their fantasies.

My daughter thinks she's a psychic and a prophet. Where does this come from?

Television and movies like to glorify bipolar psychosis as if it conferred some miraculous powers or psychic wisdom. Unfortunately, this irresponsible media treatment only worsens patients' pathologically grandiose delusions.

Am I really able to read people's minds? I feel like I can.

I have often heard of this, although I do not know where in the nervous system this experience comes from. I suggest that you ignore it for the time being until you feel better. Then check back and see if these feelings are still important to you.

Are the scary voices I am hearing for real?

Some bipolar individuals have the sense that they hear the voice of God or the devil telling them what to do. It is not a family member's or professional's place to question your spiritual beliefs; those will test themselves over time. However, many of these voices come from your subconscious mind, which contains strange and often terrifying things. It is almost like having dreams while you are still awake. My experience is that the longer people stay healthy, the less interesting these scary voices become.

I know I have some special destiny. Will I become a great world leader?

You might, but so might anyone else. Your destiny depends on what you do, not what you feel. The sooner you get healthy and stop fantasizing, the sooner you will be able to get on with your life.

I have seen several bipolar patients who believed that they were Jesus or a great world leader, often at odds with their professed religion and citizenship. Your job is not to try to figure these things out now, but rather to become healthy. When everything is calm and stable, you can return to thinking about these issues, if you still want to.

How do I know that bipolar disorder even exists and you're not making it up to control me?

That's a tough one. If you were clear and healthy, we could sit down and discuss it and you could see the reasons behind my diagnosis. However, if you are in the middle of a psychotic episode, then nothing I can say would completely reassure you. That is why I stress that you need to be working with a psychiatrist who has a good track record and whose judgment you can trust when you are sick.

Doctors keep pressuring me to take drugs. Are they all on the payroll of the pharmaceutical industry?

No. I know of no conspiracy to force people to take drugs they do not really need. Think about it. If a doctor did not genuinely believe that medications would help you, why would he or she expend all the time, energy, and discomfort of trying to convince you to do something you did not want to do? Think how much easier your doctors' lives would be if they just went along with you and said, "Everything is fine. There's nothing serious wrong with you. You don't need bipolar medications—I'll just offer you this other treatment that you will really enjoy."

How can I prevent a loved one's bipolar psychotic break from becoming a disaster?

The most you can do is to help get the person professional care. This may be from a regular doctor or it may mean admission to the hospital.

HOSPITALIZATION

When bipolar disorder becomes too severe, hospitalization becomes an issue. A brief stay in the hospital can provide an opportunity to change medications or return people to their previous medications. Sometimes, admission to a hospital is the only option when a patient's safety is concerned.

How do you know when things are so bad that someone needs to go to the hospital?

Wondering about going to the hospital is usually a good indication that it is time to go. Seek the advice of a doctor, therapist, and/or close family members.

Are there any events that predict whether someone will have to go to the hospital with bipolar disorder?

Individuals who cycle may get sick at the same time each year. If this is not the case, look for periods of sustained stress, an especially stressful life event, or physical illness as warning signs. It is usually a good sign to go to the hospital if your loved one is out of touch with reality or engaging in behavior that may be harmful to them or anyone else.

Here is one way to remember. If they are thinking about owning the Brooklyn Bridge, they can stay home. If they are about to *buy* the Brooklyn Bridge, they should start packing. If they are about to jump off the Brooklyn Bridge, call the ambulance immediately. Potential physical harm to themselves or others must always be taken seriously, even if emotional and physical outbursts are only intermittent.

Q How can I get into the psychiatric program in the hospital? I'm willing to go.

The best way is to call your doctor and ask her or him to arrange an admission. You can also call the admissions department at the hospital and request admission. Sometimes the easiest thing to do is just go to the emergency room and ask them how to enter the hospital voluntarily for psychiatric care.

Q I took my family member to the hospital but they just sent us back home. What can we do?

With hospital crowding and an influx of nonpaying patients through the emergency room, many hospitals are forced to provide minimal care. Physicians and nurses are spread thin because of high hospital costs and the incredible amount of money siphoned off by insurance companies that never goes to treat patients at all. Under these conditions, all but the most severe patients may be quickly sent home. If this happens to you, try another hospital.

Sometimes people who should be admitted are not allowed into the hospital because they do not describe their problems clearly or in ways that are relevant to their evaluators. Physicians are looking for intent, threats, or attempts to commit suicide; intent, threats, or attempts to cause violence against other people; voices telling you to hurt oneself or other people; a history of previous hospitalizations documented in available hospital records; or the inability to care for oneself because of mental or emotional disorder.

Q What exactly can they do at the hospital that can't be done at home or in the doctor's office?

Patients in a hospital can often get the focused attention of one or more doctors to evaluate their condition and to help start or strengthen a medication treatment plan. Experienced nurses help patients learn to care for themselves and are qualified to organize and carry out most of the treatment. Most hospitals have psychotherapy in groups and on an individual basis. Hospitals may also provide occupational therapy and other specialized treatment. Usually, hospitals are the best place to find out if there are concurrent physical problems that might be missed in a doctor's office, such as diabetes or a brain tumor.

Is the hospital a safe place for my suicidal daughter?

In addition to treatment, hospitals may provide a safe place for those in danger of hurting themselves or others. Sometimes the treatment under these conditions is simply to place your loved one in the hospital and wait until the crisis is over. Bear in mind that no place is truly safe for people who are determined to kill themselves. A few of my patients have even made suicide attempts in their hospital rooms.

My son is getting dangerous and needs to go to the hospital, but he will not go. What do I do?

I know of nothing you can do unless your son is in danger of harming himself or others. If that is the case, you can call Rescue/911 and ask them to come evaluate your son. If they agree that there is a danger of him hurting himself or others, the medics can usually take him to the hospital or arrange for that to happen. Alternatively, if he is committing criminal acts, his psychiatric care may be assumed by the criminal justice system.

My spouse has had bipolar disorder for years, but the hospital doctors think it's schizophrenia. Who is right?

For years, it was common practice for doctors to diagnose schizophrenia whenever hallucinations were present. Even now, when doctors say "psychotic illness" they usually mean schizophrenia, although there is just as much psychosis at work in bipolar disorder. In all fairness, the presence of psychosis makes it difficult to distinguish between schizophrenia, bipolar disorder, psychotic depression, toxicity, brain injury, or nervous system disease. Sometimes the only way to tell is to reevaluate after the psychotic period is over.

What can I do if my hospitalized spouse isn't responding to schizophrenic medications?

If his doctors will listen to your opinions, ask them to try medications that treat both bipolar disorder and schizophrenia, such as mood stabilizers and atypical antipsychotics. Then try to get another diagnostic assessment after your spouse has improved.

What can I tell my friend in the hospital to help encourage wellness? It won't work to nag him about how he should take his meds.

Visit your friend in the hospital and tell him how much happier you would be if he could work on his treatment and get well again. You may not be able to do anything more until your friend has a change of heart.

How can I keep my spouse from going back in the hospital?

Find out how frequently your spouse is seeing the doctor or medical team outside the hospital. If your spouse is not going to the doctor to work on her medications, then she will not get better. If the doctor only sees patients for a few minutes per appointment, then your spouse is unlikely to develop a good doctor/patient relationship. If your spouse refuses to take medications, then she will not get better. If you only hear a lot of excuses about why she cannot take medicine or go to the doctor, then there will not be any improvement.

How can I help my brother? He's going to be discharged from the hospital soon.

Ask for permission to talk to your brother's doctor in the hospital. Find out what the doctor thinks is the problem. Ask your brother's hospital doctor who will be seeing your brother after he leaves the hospital and confirm that he will have an outpatient appointment before he is released. Make sure that your brother has medications and/or prescriptions before he leaves the hospital.

Go to an online or local support group and talk to other family members about what they have done before their loved ones have left the hospital.

My sister has bipolar disorder that is more severe than that of most of the patients you talk about. She's always in the hospital, and she has never been able to work. How do I help her?

Meet with her doctor and social worker to confirm that she is getting all the forms of outpatient care and treatment to which she is entitled. Find out if she is eligible for federal or state programs and funds. Insist on being informed of the outpatient care planning and the means in place to keep your sister from returning to the hospital.

I had a bad experience in a hospital before. How do I know I won't have one again?

Years ago, hospitals served to provide a haven where patients could relax and take a break from their daily stresses. However, modern hospitalizations are usually brief, hurried, full of compulsory activities, and not very restful.

Providing care in most modern hospitals is quite complex, and mistakes happen. Nevertheless, most of the hospital staff I know work hard to try to make things go smoothly and comfortably for their patients.

Once the diagnosis is right, what is the main cause of treatment failure in the hospital?

Bipolar hospital patients most often fail treatment because they do not take their medications, even in the hospital. We call this "noncompliance." Patients can choose not to cooperate in their treatment if they wish. Most often, patients stick their pills in their cheeks and spit them out later when no one is looking. When I was working on hospital psychiatry wards, I would often visit the bathrooms ten minutes after medications were given. The toilet bowls were always full of bright colors from the pills patients had deposited there.

Nurses try every sort of strategy to check mouths, hands, and pockets to make sure that patients actually swallow their pills. There are even pills that dissolve almost immediately in the mouth. Nevertheless, I am convinced that hospital patients can ditch their medication if they are determined. Ultimately, treatment is the same in the hospital as it is outside; people have to want to get well or it will not happen.

While I was in medical school, I treated a middle-aged manic man who had been hospitalized frequently over many years without any improvement, despite many complex medication combinations. When my stay on the ward was done, he confided in me that he had not swallowed any medication in the past twenty years.

Are there other common causes of failure to recover after hospitalization?

I still run into plenty of sick bipolar patients who have never been given an adequate trial of a mood stabilizer. Some records will show that patients have received a mood stabilizer but the medication was given at too low a dose or for too short a time. You can look in the *Physician's Desk Reference* (PDR) or on the Internet to find the usual minimum and maximum dose and the recommended duration of treatment for any mood stabilizer.

ATTITUDES THAT MAKE IT DIFFICULT TO RECOVER FROM BIPOLAR DISORDER

. . . . . .

Over the years, I have noticed certain directions of thinking that interfere with recovery. Sometimes these attitudes predict when patients will stop their treatment altogether. Here are some examples of statements I have heard that reflect these counterproductive attitudes.

- "I don't think I have to take medications all the time."
- "I don't think my bipolar disorder is that bad."
- "I want to stop my medications to see if I really have bipolar disorder or not."
- "I just want to see what I feel like if I don't take the medicines."
- "I just want to try doing this on my own."
- "I don't want medications because they are a crutch."
- "If my willpower is strong enough, I know I can beat this without medications."
- "I want treatment but I want to start it later."
- "I still have doubts about whether I have bipolar disorder or not."
- "None of my friends think I have bipolar disorder."
- "I talked to a professional who says he is sure I don't have bipolar disorder."
- "I read in a book that I don't have to take medicines for bipolar disorder."
- "I just want to try diet and minerals first."
- "I'm sure I can't have a disease. I've never been sick in my life."
- "My problems are all because of circumstances. I have good reasons to act this way."
- "It's not my fault. It's really all the fault of my (job, wife, mother, boyfriend, house, city, country, etc.)"
- "If I can just get away from this place I know I'll be okay."
- "If I could just get to sleep (or wake up) then everything would be fine."
- "Don't you even trust me that I can handle this by myself?"
- "I don't like the doctor anymore."
- "I don't like the medicine anymore."
- "I always have good luck. Don't worry. Trust me. Things will work out just fine."

WHAT TO DO WHEN NOTHING IS WORKING

Grandiosity, fantasy, illogic, and the belief that rules and consequences do not apply to them are the greatest barriers to recovery for patients with bipolar disorder. Regardless of their fantasies, bipolar sufferers must be willing to work hard on their treatment in order to be healthy.

What is the most common cause of treatment failure in bipolar disorder?

Refusing to take medications or stopping them. Basically, medications are the only things that can normalize the thought process and block the return of mania or depression. There is evidence that the more times that you abruptly stop medications, the worse the illness becomes.

What's the most common belief that stands in the way of recovery?

"I feel fine now; therefore I don't need to take the medications." This is an error in logic but it makes sense to people in the throes of bipolar disorder. In reality, if you take the medications and feel better, then you should go on taking the medications in order to keep feeling better. If you improve, it is not because your illness has mysteriously gone away; it is because the medications are taking those disease symptoms away.

How do I know if I've given my medications enough time to work? I don't want to give up.

You really need to have at least a six-month trial of the three major mood stabilizers at moderate to high therapeutic blood levels before you can be sure that these medications will not help you. I have consulted on many patients who were said to be completely refractory to treatment who responded well after they had an adequate trial of a major mood stabilizer.

Are there ever any people who cannot be helped by any medications?

Fewer than a dozen people in my career have failed to respond to appropriate doses of medications. In most cases, these individuals had years of recurrent, uncontrolled manic episodes, alcohol, and/or substance use. A few have been younger people who had been treated with antidepressants and had a history of frequent manic episodes going back into childhood. Even in these cases, the bipolar symptoms could be reduced with medications and hard work on lifestyle changes.

What can I do when everything else fails?

This is a good time to step back and take an objective look at the reasons for the failure. Frequently treatment fails because of other health problems that are either overlooked or dismissed. For example, I have consulted on numerous cases where alcohol and/or drug use has sabotaged medical treatment efforts. When these people were able to stop using any alcohol or drugs, their medications made them well again. Sometimes the concurrent presence of brain damage or physical illness renders treatment ineffective; this is the time to repeat the physical examination. Bipolar treatment can also be sabotaged by refusal to reduce stress, go to bed at a reasonable hour, eat appropriate meals, or exercise in moderation. When these problems are discovered, they must be dealt with if there is to be any hope of achieving good treatment.

When is bipolar disorder beyond help?

Bipolar disorder is only beyond help when you give up.

10.

RESOURCES

. . . .

Ultimately, your best source of information and help will come from working with a psychiatrist and/or therapist who is experienced in treating bipolar disorder and willing to develop a close working relationship with you. However, there is a wealth of information available in your environment.

USING THE INTERNET TO FIGHT BIPOLAR DISORDER

Bipolar websites offer services such as online support groups, local and national meetings, and an opportunity to participate in the politics of health care. They also offer an opportunity to improve your own health and an opportunity for you to help others. However, there is lots of misleading and incorrect information on the Internet, and lots of people with an ax to grind, so I cannot guarantee your results. Start with major societies and institutions that have committed their service to the bipolar community and have no financial, political, or personal profit to be made. Remember that almost anyone can post on chat lines and bulletin boards, so do not give away personal information or trust all the comments. These are some of the sources I have found. In addition to Web addresses, I have tried to provide telephone numbers for most of these listings in case you want to talk to a real person.

ONLINE INTERNET FORUMS: BIPOLAR NEWS AND CHAT GROUPS

There are many Internet bulletin boards and chat groups addressing issues important to the bipolar community. To find them, try searching "bulletin board bipolar" or "chat bipolar" on a search engine like Dogpile (http://www.dogpile.com) or Google (http:www.google.com). AOL makes it easy. Just go to the "Health" page, find the "Health Talk Directory," click on "Depression," and you will see "Bipolar Disorder." Or check some of the sites below.

http://www.supportpath.com/sl_b/bipolar_disorder.htm
http://www.supportalk.com/group-8-1601.html
http://www.pendulum.org/penduforum
http://www.groups.google.com/group/alt.support.depression.manic
http://www.bipolarworld.net/Community/bplounge.htm
http://www.bipolarworld.net/Community/bpsupport.html
http://bipolar.about.com/cs/menu_chat/l/bl_chatcal.htm

ORGANIZATIONS AND THE SERVICES THEY PROVIDE

Many of the major health organizations work hard on providing services for patients. These websites can also be the starting point to join national bipolar organizations, sign up for publications, locate national and statewide conventions, and find local groups and meetings.

The American Medical Association (AMA)

This is the major organization representing all types of physicians in the United States. They offer information for doctors and patients and publish the *Journal of the American Medical Association* (JAMA) and the psychiatric journal called *Archives of Psychiatry*.

http://www.ama-assn.org
800-621-8335

The American Psychiatric Association (APA)

The website for the APA is sponsored by the premier psychiatric professional society in the United States. It provides information on psychiatric illnesses and treatment, current news, interest groups, advocacy, and ethics. They publish the *Journal of the American Psychiatric Association.*

http://www.psych.org

888-357-7924

The American Psychiatric Association Alliance

This division of the American Psychiatric Association is dedicated to patients' needs.

http://www.apaalliance.org

Angela Poblocki, Executive Director

ANG3689@aol.com

Alcoholics Anonymous (AA)

The site for AA is a clearinghouse for information on the twelve-step program and services for its members. If your bipolar disorder is complicated by alcohol or substance abuse, go here first or look in your telephone book for an AA meeting near you.

http://www.alcoholics-anonymous.org

212-870-3400

Bipolar Disorder Today

A broad website addressing several mental health conditions.

http://www.mental-health-today.com/bp/

bipolar.com

Pharmaceutical manufacturer GlaxoSmithKline supports this website. It features information on recognizing bipolar disorder, psychotherapy, building a support network, and a list of recommended books.

http://www.bipolar.com

888-825-5249

Bipolar Magazine
For twenty dollars, you can purchase a quarterly magazine devoted to individuals who have bipolar disorder. Better yet, visit their website for free. It has articles from the printed issues.

http://www.bphope.com

866-672-3038

Subscriptions: 888-834-5537

Cbel.com
An index to many professional organizations, articles, private Web pages, and even mailing lists on bipolar disorder.

http://www.cbel.com/mood_disorders/

Depression and Bipolar Support Alliance (DBSA)
Formerly the National Association for Depression and Manic Depression (NADMD), this organization shares information on support groups, speakers, advocacy, communication with lawmakers, chat, discussion, and an opportunity to share your personal story. It publishes a newsletter called *Outreach*.

http://www.dbsalliance.org

800-826-3632

Depression and Related Affective Disorders Association (DRADA)
This site is allied with the psychiatry department at Johns Hopkins University. They feature support groups, speakers, meetings, and volunteer opportunities centered in the region around Baltimore.

http://www.drada.org

410-583-2919

eMedicine Consumer Health
This private corporation specializes in mental health data and provides some information about bipolar disorder.

http://www.emedicinehealth.com

402-341-3222

International Society for Bipolar Disorders
This site is partially funded by the pharmaceutical maker Lilly.

http://www.isbd.org

412-605-1412

Madison Institute of Medicine (MIM)

A source of information on medical treatments for bipolar disorder.
http://www.miminc.org
608-827-2470

The Massachusetts General Hospital Bipolar Clinic & Research Program (MGHBCRP)

Useful information about bipolar disorder and their program.
http://www.manicdepressive.org
617-726-6188

National Association for Mental Illness (NAMI)

This organization provides information, support groups, and meetings for mental illnesses, including bipolar disorder. They support public action, advocacy, and demonstrations for the rights of persons with bipolar disorder and other mental illnesses. They also publish a magazine called *The Advocate* for members.

http://www.nami.org
800-950-6264
703-524-9094

National Mental Health Association (NMHA)

A patient who was abused by the system started this nonprofit organization. The website offers mental health information, news, and an affiliate program.

http://www.nmha.org
800-969-6642

Psychiatric Times

This online magazine supplies educational programs and up-to-date information for psychiatrists and offers a variety of information not necessarily available to the general public.

http://www.psychiatrictimes.com

Stanford University School of Medicine Bipolar Disorders Clinic

A site providing information about bipolar disorder and the treatment programs at my psychiatry alma mater.

http://bipolar.stanford.edu
650-724-4795

The World Psychiatric Association (WPA)

This psychiatric society provides international information for professionals and the public. The site contains a useful listing of university departments of psychiatry, hospitals, and mental health organizations around the world.

http://www.wpanet.org

U.S. GOVERNMENT HEALTH AND INFORMATION SERVICES

These federal websites contain so much accurate information that it is sometimes a challenge to find it all. You paid the federal government to fund national institutes and services, so you should get your money's worth.

The National Institute of Mental Health (NIMH)

This organization distributes information on mental health and mental health research as well as offering public meetings, advocacy, and access to legislation on mental health issues. This is the real thing.

http://www.nimh.nih.gov

301-443-4513

The National Institute on Drug Abuse (NIDA)

This website shares information and research on drug abuse and addiction from the major government agency devoted to the topic.

http://www.nida.nih.gov

301-443-1124

The National Mental Health Information Center (NMHIC)

This site features information on protection and advocacy, press releases, and access to information from national publications and libraries.

http://www.mentalhealth.samhsa.gov

800-789-2647

Medline

This service of the National Library of Medicine (http://www.nlm.nih.gov/) and the National Institutes of Health (http://www.nih.gov) provides searchable access to current research publications and scholarly articles on medical and clinical science for doctors, patients, and research scientists. This may be the greatest resource you have ever found.

http://medline.cos.com
Medline-related services:
http://medlineplus.gov/
http://www.paperchase.com/
http://www.ncbi.nlm.nih.gov/entrez/query.fcgi

The United States Department of Health and Human Services (USDHHS)
This site covers the heart of United States health policy.
http://www.surgeongeneral.gov
877-696-6775
202-619-0257
1-800-MEDICARE

PRIVATELY OWNED BIPOLAR WEBSITES

There are some great bipolar websites out there, waiting to be discovered. This is your opportunity to get help from your peers, check up on the latest controversies, and become part of the international bipolar community.

Bipolar Significant Others (BPSO)
A clearinghouse of information for the spouses and caretakers of those with bipolar disorder.
http://www.bpso.org

Bipolar World: A Bipolar Family
A mixed index of bipolar information.
http://www.bipolarworld.net

Dr. Ivan Goldberg's Depression Central
This New York City psychopharmacologist airs worldwide publications and opinions mixed with his own commentary.
http://www.psycom.net/depression.central.html

Dr. Wes Burgess's Website
In addition to describing my practice, my website contains professional medical articles as well as short notes that I have written on a variety of mental health issues, including bipolar disorder.
http://www.wesburgess.yourmd.com

Harbor of Refuge, Inc.

A peer support group for bipolar disorder that offers chat, discussion, diet, exercise, and other lifestyle information.

http://www.harbor-of-refuge.org

Manic-Depressives Anonymous

A twelve-step program for bipolar disorder.

http://www.manicdepressivesanon.org/

Manic Moments: A Bipolar's World

A personal website with access to publications, discussions, and personal advice from a person with bipolar disorder.

http://www.manicmoment.org

A Silver Lining

A small website with a personal touch by those with the disorder. Their advice on living with bipolar disorder sounds good to me:

> Accept the fact that we are not weak, that this is a physical illness, which causes mental problems
>
> Have proper prescription and medical management by our psychiatrist and physicians
>
> Avoid stress at all costs
>
> Get proper rest
>
> Continually educate ourselves about our illness

http://www.a-silver-lining.org

Support 4 Hope

A website with much information and many links.

http://support4hope.com/bipolar_disorder/index.htm

PROFESSIONAL BOOKS ON BIPOLAR DISORDER AND MEDICAL SCIENCE

You can find some of the same books that I use for references in university libraries, medical school bookstores, and online. Bear in mind that these are usually expensive, heavy, and full of medical jargon, and they are quite difficult to read. Here are some that I have used:

Mark Beers and Robert Brew, editors. *The Merck Manual of Diagnosis and Therapy.* John Wiley & Sons, 1999. A reasonably priced medical bible with information on all medical conditions for doctors and other medical professionals.

Jerrold G. Bernstein. *Drug Therapy in Psychiatry.* PSG Publishing Company, 1988. A nice book by the chairman of a psychiatry department where I trained.

F. K. Goodwin and K. Redfield Jamison. *Manic-Depressive Illness.* Oxford University Press, 1990.

J. G. Hardman and L. E. Limbird. *Goodman & Gilman's The Pharmacological Basis of Therapeutics.* McGraw Hill, 2001.

Eric Kandel and J. H. Schwartz. *Principles of Neural Science.* Elsevier, 1985. I think so highly of this book that I use it as a textbook when I teach neuropsychology.

B. J. Sadock and V. A. Sadock. *Kaplan & Sadock's Comprehensive Textbook of Psychiatry.* Lippincott, Williams, & Williams, 2005. A very thick resource with lots of information.

PSYCHOBIOLOGICAL AND PHILOSOPHICAL BOOKS

The following books may provide some help in describing and understanding the experience of consciousness that is so important and so puzzling in the context of bipolar disorder:

J. M. Davidson and R. J. Davidson. *The Psychobiology of Consciousness.* Plenum Press, 1982. A view into the scientific explanations of conscious experience.

Arthur M. Eastman, et al., editors. *The Norton Anthology of Poetry.* W. W. Norton & Company, 1975. You might like to look at the poem "You

Were Wearing," by Kenneth Koch. Several of my patients have commented that this poem sounds like what is going on in their heads when they are just beginning to become manic.

Julian Jaynes. *The Origin of Consciousness in the Breakdown of the Bicameral Mind.* Houghton Mifflin Company, 1976. A theory of consciousness that may be especially interesting to persons with bipolar disorder.

C. G. Jung. *Synchronicity: An Acausal Connecting Principle.* Bollingen Series. Princeton University Press, 1973. A brief treatise attempting to explain the unexplainable in a clear and logical way.

J. Krishnamurti. *Commentaries on Living.* First, Second, and Third Series. Quest Books, 1973. These readable volumes address a variety of practical issues while demonstrating a philosophy of insight and objectivity.

Robert Pirsig. *Zen and the Art of Motorcycle Maintenance.* Harper and Row, 1975. I used to keep a stockpile of these books so I could give them out to my friends. If you have not read it, do so.

Paul Reps, editor. *Zen Flesh, Zen Bones.* Charles E. Tuttle, 1990. Reps has collected material from three books and an article from *Gentry* magazine to illustrate Zen thought. If you are tired of struggling with the rigid, linear Western style of thinking then you may find this book entertaining.

John Beer, editor. *Samuel Taylor Coleridge: Poems.* Everyman/Charles E. Tuttle, 1995. Of all poets, I think that Coleridge speaks most strongly with the bipolar voice.

E. H. Warmington and P. G. Rouse, editors. *Great Dialogues of Plato.* New American Library, 1956. Plato addresses many topics as the mouthpiece of his mentor Socrates, whom some suspect may have been bipolar.

Ludwig Wittgenstein. *Zettel.* Edited by G. E. M. Anscombe and G. H. von Wright. University of California Press, 1976. This is a very accessible volume of short thoughts by Wittgenstein on the philosophical outlook that he originated called logical positivism.

BIPOLAR AND HEALTH BOOKS
FOR THE GENERAL READER

I rarely find a nonprofessional book on psychiatry or mental health that I like wholeheartedly. However, use your own judgment and try to take the best from whatever you read. Here are some titles:

Mark H. Beers, Editor. *The Merck Manual of Medical Information.* Pocket Books, 2003. The popular version of a major book on all things medical.

Patty Duke, Mary Lou Pinkert, and Gloria Hochman. *A Brilliant Madness.* Bantam Books, 1993.

Jan Fawcett, Bernard Golden, Nancy Rosenfeld, Boris Birmaher, and Frederick Goodwin. *New Hope for People with Bipolar Disorder.* Prima Publishing, 2000.

Roger Granet and Elizabeth Ferber. *Why Am I Up, Why Am I Down? Understanding Bipolar Disorder.* Dell Publishing Co, 1999.

Kay Redfield Jamison. *An Unquiet Mind: A Memoir of Moods and Madness.* Random House, 1997.

Kay Redfield Jamison. *Touched with Fire: Manic-Depressive Illness and the Artistic Temperament.* Touchstone Books, 1993, 1996.

David Miklowitz. *The Bipolar Disorder Survival Guide.* Guilford Press, 2002.

Francis Mondimore. *Bipolar Disorder: A Guide for Patients and Families.* Johns Hopkins Press Health Book, 1999.

E. F. Torrey and Michael Knable. *Surviving Manic Depression.* Basic Books, 2002.

Lizzie Simon. *Detour: My Bipolar Road Trip in 4-D.* Pocket Star Press, 2002.

Mitzi Waltz. *Adult Bipolar Disorders: Understanding Your Diagnosis and Getting Help.* O'Reilly & Associates, 2002.

Epilogue

The most important advice for being healthy and successful with bipolar disorder is that you should be objective about all things. Most of the problems of bipolar disorder are founded on fantasies and distortions. Pessimism is a distortion of reality in a negative direction. Overoptimism is a distortion of reality in a positive direction. Grandiosity is a distorted exaggeration of your own importance. Low self-esteem is a distorted exaggeration of your own unimportance. Paranoia is a distorted exaggeration of your fears. Unfounded jealousy is a distortion of your feelings of undesirability. Rage is a distortion of your need to blame others for your own shortcomings. Psychosis is a distortion of your true experience of the world. Fantasies are only illusions: they sap your energy and creativity and impede you from having the kind of life you want and deserve. As you view the world with greater objectivity, you will enjoy better health and get more of what you want out of your life. If you do just one thing, work on being truthful, honest, and objective with yourself.

Appendix A

THE OFFICIAL DSM-IV DIAGNOSTIC CRITERIA FOR MANIA AND ATYPICAL DEPRESSION

The American Psychiatric Association's *Diagnostic and Statistical Manual of Mental Disorders, Fourth Edition (DSM-IV-TR),* diagnostic criteria for *mania* are as follows:

A. A distinct period of abnormally and persistently elevated, expansive, and/or irritable mood, lasting at least one week (or any duration if hospitalization is necessary).

B. During the period of mood disturbance, three (or more) of the following symptoms have persisted (four if the mood is only irritable) and have been present to a significant degree:

1. inflated self-esteem or grandiosity
2. a decreased need for sleep (e.g., feels rested after only three hours of sleep)
3. more talkative than usual or pressure to keep talking
4. flight of ideas or subjective experience that thoughts are racing
5. distractibility (i.e., attention too easily drawn to unimportant or irrelevant external stimuli)
6. increase in goal-directed activity (either socially, at work or school, or sexually) or psychomotor agitation
7. excessive involvement in pleasurable activities that have a high po-

tential for painful consequences (e.g., engaging in unrestrained buying sprees, sexual indiscretions, or foolish business investments)
C. The symptoms do not meet criteria for a Mixed [Bipolar] Episode.
D. The mood disturbance is sufficiently severe to cause marked impairment in
occupational functioning or in usual social activities or relationships with
others or to necessitate hospitalization to prevent harm to self or others, or
there are psychotic features.
E. The symptoms are not due to the direct physiological effects of a substance
(e.g., a drug of abuse, a medication, or other treatment) or a general medical condition (e.g., hyperthyroidism).

The American Psychiatric Association's *Diagnostic and Statistical Manual of Mental
Disorders, Fourth Edition (DSM-IV-TR),* diagnostic criteria for *depression with atypical
features* are as follows:

With atypical features (can be applied when these features predominate during
the most recent two weeks of a current Major Depressive Episode in Major Depressive Disorder or in Bipolar I or Bipolar II Disorder when a current Major Depressive Episode is the most recent type of mood episode, or when these features
predominate during the most recent two years of Dysthymic Disorder; if the Major Depressive Episode is not current, it applies if the feature predominates during
any two-week period)

A. Mood reactivity (i.e., mood brightens in response to actual or potential positive events)
B. Two (or more) of the following features:
    1. significant weight gain or increase in appetite
    2. hypersomnia
    3. leaden paralysis (i.e., heavy, leaden feelings in arms or legs)
    4. long-standing pattern of interpersonal rejection sensitivity (not lim-
       ited to episodes of mood disturbance) that results in significant social
       or occupational impairment
C. Criteria are not met With Melancholic Features or With Catatonic Features
during the same episode.

Appendix B

THE NATIONAL INSTITUTE OF MENTAL HEALTH LIST OF THE SYMPTOMS OF MANIA, COMBINED BIPOLAR AND UNIPOLAR DEPRESSION, AND PSYCHOSIS

Signs and symptoms of *mania* include:

- Increased energy, activity, and restlessness
- Excessively "high," overly good, euphoric mood
- Extreme irritability
- Racing thoughts and talking very fast, jumping from one idea to another
- Distractibility, can't concentrate well
- Little sleep needed
- Unrealistic beliefs in one's abilities and powers
- Poor judgment
- Spending sprees
- A lasting period of behavior that is different from usual
- Increased sexual drive
- Abuse of drugs, particularly cocaine, alcohol, and sleeping medications
- Provocative, intrusive, or aggressive behavior
- Denial that anything is wrong

A manic episode is diagnosed if elevated mood occurs with three or more of the other symptoms most of the day, nearly every day, for one week or longer. If the mood is irritable, four additional symptoms must be present.

Signs and symptoms of [bipolar and unipolar] *depression* include:

- Lasting sad, anxious, or empty mood
- Feelings of hopelessness or pessimism
- Feelings of guilt, worthlessness, or helplessness
- Loss of interest or pleasure in activities once enjoyed, including sex
- Decreased energy, a feeling of fatigue or of being "slowed down"
- Difficulty concentrating, remembering, making decisions
- Restlessness or irritability
- Sleeping too much, or can't sleep
- Change in appetite and/or unintended weight loss or gain
- Chronic pain or other persistent bodily symptoms that are not caused by physical illness or injury
- Thoughts of death or suicide, or suicide attempts

A depressive episode is diagnosed if five or more of these symptoms last most of the day, nearly every day, for a period of two weeks or longer.

Common symptoms of *psychosis* include:

- Hallucinations—hearing, seeing, or otherwise sensing the presence of things not actually there
- Delusions—false, strongly held beliefs not influenced by logical reasoning or explained by a person's usual cultural concepts

Psychotic symptoms in bipolar disorder tend to reflect the extreme mood state at the time. For example, delusions of grandiosity, such as believing one is the president or has special powers or wealth, may occur during mania; delusions of guilt or worthlessness, such as believing that one is ruined and penniless or has committed some terrible crime, may appear during [unipolar major] depression. People with bipolar disorder who have [psychotic] symptoms are sometimes incorrectly diagnosed as having schizophrenia, another severe mental illness.

From National Institute of Mental Health, *Bipolar Disorder.*
http://www.nimh.nih.gov/publicat/bipolar.cfm, Bethesda (MD): National Institute of Mental Health, National Institutes of Health, U.S. Department of Health and Human Services, 2001.

Author's Note

Case histories and other patient-related material are made up of a composite of similar cases whose details have been altered so that no example in this book refers to or can be identified with any person living or dead. This book does not constitute an endorsement or recommendation of any products or services mentioned in the text. This book is not a substitute for professional guidance; please discuss the issues in this book with your doctor. In all cases, use your own best judgment and that of your doctor and therapist to determine which comments in this book will work the most safely and effectively for you.

Index